TABLE OF CONTENTS

TO PROD THE "SLUMBERING GIANT"

Crisis, Commitment, and Christian Education

Essays by

John Vriend
James H. Olthuis
John C. VanderStelt
Harro Van Brummelen
John Van Dyk
Adrian Peetoom
John A. Olthuis

Other titles from Wedge with similar contents include

Cultural Objectives for the Christian Teacher *by Calvin G. Seerveld*
Insight, Authority and Power *by Peter A. Schouls*
The Necessity of Christian Universities *by J.D. Dengerink*
A Place to Stand (a case for public support for ALL public schools)
by John A. Olthuis
The Relation of the Bible to Learning *by H. Evan Runner*

 Wedge Publishing Foundation, 229 College St.,
Toronto 2B, Ontario, Canada. M5T 1R4

Copyright 1972© Wedge Publishing Foundation, Toronto, Canada. Printed
by General Printers, Oshawa, Ontario. Cover Design by Terry Black

CONTRIBUTORS

Harro Van Brummelen is principal of the Edmonton Christian High School in Edmonton, Alberta; his responsibilities include teaching mathematics there. He has led several summer workshops in mathematics education, and is the editor of the resulting publication, *Mathematics in the Christian School*. His articles on education have been published in several magazines, particularly in the *Christian School Herald*.

John Van Dyk teaches history at Dordt College in Sioux Center, Iowa. He is secretary of the national board of the National Association for Christian Political Action (NACPA). He has written several articles, including "The Enemy Within: Secularism in Christian Education," "Christ or Chaos," and "A Practical/Obedient Program for Christian Political Action." He is well known for his classroom syllabi in history; two of these are *Survey of the History of Philosophy* and *A Christian Approach to Medieval History*. His essay, "From Deformation to Reformation," appeared in *Will All the King's Men*, a collection of essays on reformation in the Church.

James H. Olthuis teaches ethics and theology at the Institute for Christian Studies in Toronto. He's written several seminal papers which are in stencilled and pamphlet form; these include *Ambiguity is the Key*, "Values and Valuation," "The Reality of Societal Structures," "The World of God and Science," and "The Word of God and Hermeneutics." He is the author of *Facts, Values and Ethics,* published in 1969. With Gerald Vandezande he is coauthor of *'Bunglers and Visionaries': Christian Labour at the Crossroads*. With Bernard Zylstra he wrote "Confessing Christ in Education" and "Schools in the Christian Community." He is the author of many published articles, and contributed an essay to *Will All the King's Men*, entitled "Worship and Witness."

John A. Olthuis is executive director of the Association for the Advancement of Christian Scholarship (AACS) and is active in the CJL Foundation, a Canadian Christian civil rights organization. Besides providing leadership for a number of projects and organizations, he has been an active author. His pamphlet, *A Place to Stand* (a case for public support for *all* public schools), has received wide distribution in Canada and the U.S. Contributions to books include essays in *Out of Concern for the Church, Hope for the Family,* and *Will all the King's Men.* He has been a columnist and feature writer for Vanguard Magazine.

Adrian Peetoom represents an educational publishing company in Western Canada, as salesman and field editor. He has served on educational committees and boards of Christian schools, and was a member of the board and educational committee of the Ontario Alliance of Christian Schools. He has contributed two series of articles to *Calvinist-Contact* under the titles, "Parents and Children," and "Schools and Covenants." His work in educational publishing over the last ten years has given him a unique vantage point for evaluating what is happening in North American education. And as he observes, "What I have learned in schools compels me to have a close look at what I do as a parent." As his wife observes, "I hope you know what you're doing!"

John C. VanderStelt teaches philosophy and theology at Dordt College, Sioux Center, Iowa. A number of his articles and addresses have been published in various magazines. Articles include "Church in Society: An Orientation"; "Christian Action and Sphere Sovereignty"; "Christian Involvement and the Word"; "The Struggle of Calvinism in North America"; "Integration of Scriptural Principles and Science in General," and "Revelation: Harmony versus Conflict." His article, "Kuyper's Semi-Mysticism," has been included in a *Festschrift* for Dr. D.H. Th. Vollenhoven, the eminent Dutch Christian historian of philosophy.

John Vriend is pastor of the First Christian Reformed Church of Edmonton, Alberta. He has served pastorates in Montreal, Quebec; Simcoe, Ontario; and Lethbridge, Alberta. He has written numerous articles on education, worship, and politics; he is the author of two booklets of meditations: "Sidelights in Scripture" and "In the Sanctuary of Death". He is the father of seven children; their educations have impressed upon him the necessity of Christian day school nurture.

PREFACE

During the past two decades an unprecedented number of Christian day schools have been opened in North America, and throughout the English-speaking world. And yet the number of children enrolled in these fledgling institutions of Christian learning is only a small fraction of all children of Christian families. Meanwhile the secular humanist "public" schools have been listing from crisis to crisis and the earlier pagan consensus about the proper kind of education for the democratic state has collapsed. Most Christian parents have never heard of Charles Silberman or his book entitled, *Crisis in the Classroom,* and the seriousness of the educational situation has never dawned on them.

This is a volume concerned about the contemporary educational crisis, about the many proposed solutions which have been given by secular thinkers, but more specially it is aimed at prodding the "slumbering giant," the Christian community, into realizing the crisis of commitment which confronts us when we consider how our children ought to be nurtured in the light of the Scriptures. And this book is about the challenging alternatives of Christian day school education.

The following questions are asked and answered in essays fashioned by seven educational leaders attuned to Biblical solutions: Why do we need Christian schools? Won't that be like stuffing Christianity down our children's throats? Why aren't the Christian schools already established supported by the whole Christian community? How good are these schools? Why is there such confusion about what Christian schools should do -- are they primarily for evangelism? for a Christian atmosphere, for protecting our kids from the world, or for teaching them to be citizens of God's Kingdom -- which of these ideals is best? What is my personal responsibility in my own community? All these and other questions and issues are raised and dealt with.

The seven essays of *To Prod the "Slumbering Giant"* were originally given as 1971-72 Discovery lectures on behalf of the international Association for the Advancement of Christian Scholarship (AACS); they have been chosen from a large number of manuscripts to form the best possible unity, combining qualities of wisdom, insight and inspiration.

i

John Vriend and James H. Olthuis consider the place and task of Christian education in Biblical perspective; the struggle for Christian education in western history is delineated by John C. VanderStelt; Harro Van Brummelen and John Van Dyk treat the topic of curriculum design as a guideline in Christ-centered living and learning; how to organize the school for learning is developed by Adrian Peetoom; and the place of the Christian school in North American society is the subject of a last chapter written by John A. Olthuis. The seven essays are contained in five chapters arranged to give a sequential order to various phases and facets of the subject matter. For more information about the authors a list of contributors is provided.

These essays go to the heart of the present debate about what education should be and do. The alternative of Christian education through the vehicle of day schools is cogently presently and convincingly argued. A challenge is clearly presented throughout the book to all those who are interested in struggling with their fellow believers to take their educational responsibilities seriously. Make no mistake about it -- the issues are crucial for both those who are contemplating Christian schools for the first time and for those who may be wondering if their commitment to them is still worth the sacrifice. As John Olthuis writes in the book's last chapter, "I believe that Christian schools have a crucial role to play in the emergence of public Christianity because they must educate the persons who will make it possible. Since different educational goals reflect different societal goals, a different Christian educational system will be needed to adapt to the evolving humanistic culture than to support the emergence of public Christianity. Christian schools provide the link between the present society and the possibilities for the emergence of a different type of society."

The kind of Christian schools which emerge in coming years, or whether the present Christian schools will even survive will in part depend on your response and contribution to the great debate that is clearly present throughout this book. If you are helped to make up your mind about the crucial issues by reading part or all of *To Prod the "Slumbering Giant"*, then the publication of this book will have been well worth the effort.

Robert Lee Carvill
Toronto

1

THE PLACE AND TASK OF
CHRISTIAN EDUCATION
IN BIBLICAL PERSPECTIVE

No Neutral Ground: Why I'm Committed to Christian Education

by John Vriend

The word that strikes the eye as you scan the title of books on Education in any public library is *Crisis*. *Crisis in the Classroom* is the title, not of one book only but, in substance at least, of several. That is remarkable because, according to the writers of these same books, schools occupy neutral ground. They carry out their business in a supposedly trouble-free area where partisans on all *other* issues – like the religious, political, social, economic – can join in a common effort for the education of tomorrow's adults. This neutral ground of common facts and a common future is declared, in the next breath, to be sacred ground, for here everyone *can* get together, indeed *must* get together with complete understanding and support. Still crisis? Yes – a dollar crisis, a learning crisis, a human crisis. For exactly what must we be doing in these schools?

The Crisis of Reason and Personality

A century ago the champions of humanism said, "Let us teach children the undoubted results of science and scholarship. Let us discipline them into accepting a body of facts." The teachers proceeded to force concepts into the heads of little children, concepts that could be hooked

1

together in logical fashion. The *concept* began to dominate the *thing.* Live leghorns were brought into the classroom to illustrate the concept "chicken." The producer of cackleberries was then analyzed in terms of bones, muscle, fat and feathers to yield the further notion of "bird." You see what happened. Children were not introduced into God's highly diversified world of fascinating creatures; but God's creatures were used to illustrate the abstract classifications of men. It was human thought that was glorified. It was the human power of conceptualization the children were being asked to adore, not God's big creation.

The result was a colossal bore. Spartan discipline had to be used to keep the youngsters in line. Silence was the rule and rote memory the method. School was a prison house and the inmates an intellectual slave gang. Natural interest in the world around the children was systematically destroyed and their minds mutilated.

In this stultifying world of the schools a reaction was bound to set in. Academic theorists came forward to champion the *freedom* of the child. Let the child do his thing. Let him develop his own projects. Let him progress at his own pace. Let him be his own authority and set his own goals. Let the school be child-oriented, rather than curriculum-centred. Let the teacher be the stimulator and helper of the learning child, rather than the domineering force-feeder of a mass of facts and concepts. So the pendulum swung here and there from the ideal of comprehensive *knowledge* of the world to the ideal of the *freedom* of the child; from a heavy handed emphasis on the content of the curriculum to anxious concern about the progress of the individual child.

There can be no doubt that the swing from the body of facts to the mastered to the liberation of the child's mind was, in fact, a release from bondage. Initially the innovators were more successful than the traditionalists.

No Neutral Ground: Why I'm Committed to the Christian School

Educators were amazed to see the results of a method which allowed children to follow the bent of natural curiosity. To think that a child would investigate a period of history of its own accord or make its own natural-history collection of eggs, or leaves, or shells! Unheard of!

A universal characteristic of nearly all schools, Christian and humanistic, past and present, seems to be a heavy preoccupation with order and control. One of the severest and most impartial means of control is, of course, the clock to which the bell is wired. It insures that things happen not because teachers want them to happen or because the students want them to happen but because it is time for them to happen. Let me give some examples. A scholar examining the curriculum of a given school arrives a few minutes early to discover that a cluster of children are standing with intense fascination around a turtle. The bell rings. "Now children, put away the turtle," says the teacher. "We're going to have our science lesson." The lesson is on crabs. Inflexible order prevails over the learning process.

From my own childhood in a Christian school I remember, with painful vividness, the day that Princess Beatrix was born. The local novelist K. Norel, who had a heart for children, had gone to the school as soon as he heard the news, rushed from one classroom to another, and shouted it out to the children inside. We immediately roared out our happiness. The House of Orange was not about to disappear from the scene. Imagine our horror when we looked up to see that the teacher – grim-faced with pencil in hand – was busy taking down the names of all the children who were shouting, and began to threaten them with appropriate punishment for breaking the rule of silence. What the teacher was saying is that history as it happens is not important; it only becomes important when

John Vriend

it is reduced to a few facts and dates in a schoolbook, which can be mastered. Knowledge of the barest and most bloodless sort is important: let history be hanged. This is the lesson even children in Christian schools seem to have learned best cf all.

A parallel instance occurred in schools in November 1963. Teachers everywhere were registering the same complaint: "I can't get the children to concentrate on their work; all they want to do is talk about the assassination of the President." The idea that children might learn more from discussing this event or that, like most adults, they were simply too obsessed with the horror of it to think of much else, did not occur to these teachers. It simply wasn't in the lesson plan. The lesson plan, logical, unemotional, compulsory, overruled the convulsions of a stunned nation in mourning. The children were shut off from the humanizing influence of this awful event in God's lesson plan. (Cf. Charles Silberman, *Crisis in the Classroom,* p. 124 ff.)

Combine this concern for order as an end in itself with the humanistic pretense of religious neutrality in the classroom, and you have the perfect formula for failure. Lightning and thunder are simply and exclusively natural phcnomcna to bc rcduccd to scicntific cquations. Lct no one think that God's majesty is revealed in the voice of the thunder or the flash of lightning. With a bit of high school science equipment you can make your own thunderstorm. Hurray for science, for man's control over nature, for his reduction of all things to that which is rational and conceptual. You are an emotional fool if you let go with "o-oh's" and "a-ah's" over the turbulence and fireworks in the sky. Until reality outside is streamlined into data you can feed into the sum total of human knowledge, it isn't fit to wonder at.

The humanist dilemma is always and forever that it

must oscillate between the pride of human reason and the pride of human personality. For if you shift from sacrificing the child to the sovereign curriculum to sacrificing the curriculum to the sovereign child, you will be not much further ahead. As Christian people we shall have to learn to see through this educational impotence of humanism. It leads inevitably to the dullness and apathy that characterizes so many graduates of the public schools. They seem to have missed completely the fascination and excitement of living and learning as God's creatures in this world. The end is intellectual death, a total blackout of the goals of life, which are, in a unique fashion, the goals of education.

It was a sad, sad student who wrote for a fine arts magazine published by a junior college the poem called "Insignificance." It goes like this:

With little trace this body fades to death
No revelation comes to meet this end.
The throat, so dry, belabors parting breath,
Blood spurts from wounds it failed to defend.
The dimming eyes and leaden hands will try
No more to seek deceptive sanctity.
The body stills; its mouth so dry, awry,
A corpse to fertilize eternity.
This minute precedent in Laws of Things,
Is produce raised in sixty years of toil
While those who preach had cried for rights and wrongs,
The fact stood . . . ideologies to foil.
The rule of nature has no consciousness,
So change from life to death is meaningless.

It is this profound pessimism that comes out, not uncharacteristically, at the end of the process of an education on which the nation spends billions of dollars. But may I ask, what else can humanism produce with its cult of human science and human personality? What but a world empty of God, a world made anxious by confrontation   after confrontation between sovereign individuals and sovereign nations none of whom wish to be subject to laws not of man's making?

The Crisis of Individualism

Humanism confronts us in our day with two major educational philosophies — collectivism and individualism. The first is the system the Marxists are perfecting. It is completely at the service of an atheistic state that seeks in every way possible to produce men and women who will carry out its policies without openly asking questions. Conformity to the ideology of the state is the sole guideline for educators, and individual initiative among students is frowned on as deviationist. The aim of the system is mass manipulation and the result, for all but a few heroic non-conformists, is intellectual slavery.

In the West we have the individualist version of humanism. "In our society," says Sterling McMurrin, "education concerns first the well-being of the individual pupil and student, his capabilities for a productive and happy life in which he can pursue an interesting and satisfying vocation." (*The Schools and the Challenge of Innovation,* p. 7.) The student must be equipped to make a living and to take part in the social, political, and cultural activities of the nation. Any goals beyond this are up to himself. The system must ignore such first-order questions as the nature and destiny of man, problems of authority and freedom, the place and task of the church in society, the absolutes of Christian morality, the possibility and reality of the forgiveness of sins. Its highly prized religious neutrality (in fact, its unblushing secular humanism) forces it to abstain from taking positions considered controversial. Meanwhile, many teachers in the public school system surreptitiously or openly scorn Christian

answers to society's needs and have no sympathy
whatsoever for a plurality of schools.

The Biblical Necessity of Nurturing

It is in this context that we are asked to listen to the
Word of the Lord. The Bible puts things in perspective. In
numerous ways it posits the *necessity of nurturing* our
children. The heart of Christian education, in biblical
language, is education of the heart. The prayer of the saint
is consistently, "O Lord, give me a heart of wisdom." It
does not hesitate to say that the fear of the Lord, awe and
reverence ("shaking in your boots") before our Creator,
Lawgiver, and Redeemer, is the first principle in gaining
any real wisdom. (Prov. 9:10, Ps. 111:10) Wisdom has to
do with the practical insight that can guide human
conduct, with the goals of living, the perils of life, the
behavior of a believing man as a member of a community
of believers. Wisdom, certainly, rather than the mere
accumulation of theoretical knowledge, must be the goal
of Christian education.

To understand the child, the Christian school is
concerned, rather *more* than other schools, with opening
his eyes to the world in which we live. That world is both
the product of, and the stage for, the works of God. These
works of God form the basic materials for the testimony
of Scripture. The Bible, therefore, consistently turns our
attention outward to that world which God has created. It
directs our mental processes, not first of all to the
conceptual activities of other people, but to the creative
activities of God. It points outwards and upwards and all
around to what God in his wisdom is doing, for example,
in nature. A Psalm like Psalm 104 is filled with "o-oh's"
and "a-ah's" over the diversity of God's creatures. "O
Lord, how manifold are thy works! In wisdom hast thou

made them all; the earth is *full* of thy creatures." (Ps. 104:24) Nor are the Psalms infected by a narrow pietism that sees *only* the works of God, but they celebrate in the same breath the cultural achievements of man. The composers gaze in awe at the sea around them and the Leviathans that cruise and tumble through its waters for their amusement; but no less at the human creations that sail over its surface. (Ps. 104:25, 26)

One of the most remarkable compositions in the Bible is Psalm 8. Obviously, this is not the place to offer a detailed introduction to it. But I cannot help showing you the unity of its theme. The psalmist is struck by a paradox. On the one hand man is but a thing of dirt — why should He who made the splendours of the skies bother with this little fellow? On the other, this tiny dirt-man occupies a unique position in the world. He has been *given* (note: he did not usurp it!) the job of being the cultural architect and manager of this planet! Talk of trust! The paradox of man's misery and majesty, so important to the business of education, would seem to threaten the unity of the psalmist's witness. But have no fears. The Psalm opens *and* closes with the identical "o-oh's" and "a-ah's" before the marvelous NAME of God which we have heard before. Skyscrapers and hydroelectric systems do not for a moment obscure that Name. They serve rather to enhance the Name of the Company for which we human beings work, whether we want to be on the payroll or not. It is the privilege of the Christian school to articulate the unity of the theme, and to express the wonder of it, in its day-by-day association with the children. Humanism might be attracted to the contents of that Psalm; in fact, it can neither grant the derivative status of man nor the beauty of the Name expressed in the *combination* of divine *and* human works.

I come now more explicitly to the scene of human

No Neutral Ground: Why I'm Committed to the Christian School

history — that to which our social and historical studies provide an introduction. Again, neither the fixed curriculum can be the norm before which all else in the school must bow, nor the sovereign pupil in his freedom. But both curriculum and child have their focus in the works of God in history. After Psalm 104 comes Psalm 105 with its even deeper and more full-throated appreciation of the accomplishments of the Redeemer-Creator. In Psalm 105 we are confronted with a double sequence of events, in all of which the God of Israel is the chief Actor. There are, on the one hand, God's *judgments* which strike down the self-inflated opposers of His will. These enemies may be the Egyptians or the Canaanites. But His judgments also come down on Israel itself. When Israel breaks faith with its Lord, He pours out His anger on His own people. On the other hand, there is the record of His *saving acts* by which again and again, Israel was rescued from its enemies. This two-sided history of judgment and of mercy is not a matter of good fortune and bad, but a drama shaped by the interaction between a holy Partner and an unholy one. The character of God shines out in the midst of human effort and human failure. *History itself is education.* "Know then in your heart that as a man disciplines his son, the Lord your God disciplines you. So you shall keep the commandments of the Lord your God, by walking in his ways and by fearing Him." (Deut. 8:5,6) "And consider . . . the discipline of the Lord your God, his greatness, his mighty hand, and his outstretched arm, his signs and his deeds." (Deut. 11:2,3)

Just as history itself disciplines God's people, so the telling of it educates their children. Again and again in Scripture, monuments are erected at historical sites to instruct later generations. The environment itself was made into a means of education. From these givens we may infer the importance of history for the Christian school as a

9

subject of instruction; certainly the importance of the *history* of *redemption* which is the core of world history.

This concern brings me to the church. A field that is almost totally neglected in the public school is the church in its day-by-day struggles, services, and mission. What opportunities for education the Christian school possesses in its close association with the Christian church! Every Sunday most of its pupils attend worship; every Monday the children come back to school with a whirl of new impressions in their heads. A baptism occurs – can the children explain this sacrament to each other in Bible class the next day? A sermon is preached – can youngsters write essays on the impressions they received of the service – favourable and unfavourable?

One day I received in the mail a manila envelope full of drawings. The drawings came from a school that was located near the church where I had preached the Sunday before. When the teacher tried to discuss the sermon with the children, they asked if instead they might draw pictures of what they had heard. So the sermon turned into an art lesson. The point is that the church and the sermon were real to the children and so they wanted to reproduce this reality in their drawings and writing. I just cannot imagine a Christian school that neglects the church in its literature, language, art, and history classes. But it is only a Christian school with a biblical view of the church that can take advantage of its close association with the church.

The glory of the Christian school is its freedom to explore the works of the Lord in nature, history, human culture, and in the world about us. Its importance lies in the fact that this exploration and the nurture that goes with it have a goal – the goal of preparing students, in the manner of the school, for living a full-orbed Christian life.

No Neutral Ground: Why I'm Committed to the Christian School

Now of that Christian life we had better have a clear conception.

A Christian Life in Faith

1. It is first of all, you will grant me, a life of faith. Not a life which includes faith as *one* element but a life which as a whole expresses faith in the Lord Jesus Christ. It is not a life composed of religious activities alongside of non-religious activities but a life in which God is gratefully served and honoured in *all* activities. It is a life with the style of a steeple – it points away and beyond itself; it is a life in which discipleship, self-denial and cross-bearing are expressed in a cultural context; a life of trust in the Lord in all circumstances, of joy in the Lord in all situations. For this kind of life, the school is the training ground.

Of course this life is much easier to describe than to live, in school or outside of school. Who of us, parents, teachers, or pupils, is equal to this religion with so many "alls" in it? Who of us is prepared to give up everything when the call comes? Yet this is the life called Christian; and for this we train our students.

A Christian Life in Community

2. But there is more. That Christian life is also a life in community. All schools, make no mistake about it, all schools induct their trainees into some kind of community. The public school under government direction, is concerned with inducting its students into the life of the nation. Our schools induct, or ought to induct, their pupils into the life of the Christian community. That community is not limited to one ethnic group; it cuts across all ethnic lines. It includes people of many different national backgrounds. Nor is it limited to the members of

John Vriend

one denomination. It includes the members of many denominations. It includes all those whose allegiance is to Jesus Christ as Lord and whose life is aimed at service for His Kingdom. That community is called the communion of saints. One of our catechisms teaches us that its members are sharers in all of Christ's gifts, including the gifts of knowledge and wisdom He bestows; it also teaches us the obligation of employing these gifts readily and cheerfully to the advantage and salvation of the other members of that community. The Christian school trains its students for this kind of sharing, a sharing that goes far beyond the boundaries of one denomination.

A Christian Life Working at Culture

3. There's more. The Christian life is life-in-community that works at culture in the name of the Lord. Christians do not isolate themselves from Canadian or American society in ethnic ghettoes of their own. Nor do they immerse themselves in their national society as if it were already sanctified. But they work at the renewal of that culture, its use of natural resources, its literature and art, its politics and economics, in the spirit of *anticipation, not negativism* – the spirit of those who anticipate a new heaven and a new earth. What alternative do such people have but to operate schools that serve as the training ground for the children who will, in some fashion and by the grace of God, have a share in reshaping the culture in which they live?

Training children, in the manner of the school, for living the Christian life; this life lived as a life of faith and in Christian community; this life as a life of community that toils at the transformation of culture, the whole of it governed by a vision, no doubt a partial vision, of the Kingdom of God – *this* is the purpose of our Christian school.

12

No Neutral Ground: Why I'm Committed to the Christian School

No Neutral Ground

To this school I am committed — today more than ever before. It grieves me that such a large number of Christians do not share this vision and are not so committed. But I have hope. I hope that in the coming decade, as the public schools reveal more unmistakably their humanist bias, more and more Christians will discover that there is no neutral ground or common ground on which to stand in the business of educating their children.

To Prod the "Slumbering Giant"

by James H. Olthuis

I can think of no better way of beginning our discussion of the nature and place of Christian education than quoting from Charles Silberman's *Crisis in the Classroom.*

> To study American education in this last third of the twentieth century is to be struck by a paradox. On the one hand, the system would appear to be in grave trouble, with the very concept of public education coming under question, from critics on the left as well as on the right. [1]

Silberman himself is most indignant about the mutilation of the child's spirit which he observed in the public schools:

> "It is not possible to spend any prolonged periods visiting public school classrooms without being appalled by the mutilation everywhere – mutilation of spontaneity, of joy in learning, of pleasure in creating, of sense of self. The public schools – those 'killers of the dream,' to appropriate a phrase of Lillian Smith's – are the kind of institution one cannot readily dislike until one gets to know them well. Because adults take the schools so much for granted, they fail to appreciate what grim, joyless places most American schools are, how oppressive and petty are the rules by which they are governed, how intellectually sterile and aesthetically barren the atmosphere, what an appalling lack of civility obtains on the part of teachers and principals, what contempt they unconsciously display for children as children."
> "And yet from another perspective, the United States educational system appears to be superbly successful – on

James H. Olthuis

> almost any measure, performing better than it did ten, twenty,
> fifty or a hundred years ago."

Why then, Silberman asks, and we with him, the present crisis? How can one explain the fact that "an educational system that appears to be superbly successful from one standpoint appears to be in grave trouble from another? The question," Silberman says, "cannot be answered with regard to education alone; it is, in fact the central paradox of American life. In almost every area, improvements beyond what anyone thought possible fifty or twenty-five or even ten years ago have produced anger and anxiety rather than satisfaction." Later he adds, "Yet contemporary technology has contributed to a pervasive sense of helplessness and impending doom at the same time that it has evoked expectations of nirvana."

> "Affluence plus new technology frees men from slavery to the
> struggle of existence. . .; it thereby forces them to confront the
> questions of life's meaning and purpose even while it destroys
> the faith that once provided the answers. Our anxiety is of the
> spirit."

In short, "the crisis is real, involving as it does the most basic questions of meaning and purpose – the meaning and purpose of life itself. It may well be a religious or spiritual crisis of a depth and magnitude that has no parallel since the Reformation."

I. The Present Crisis

It's difficult to squirm out from under the weight of these remarks. We must face them. . .Certainly we who confess the Name of Christ – believers who've promised to bring up our children in the fear and admonition of the Lord – must come to grips with this situation. Ironically, it is the Humanists today, Silberman among others, who are most concerned about this grave matter. Are Christians always going to sleep through emergencies?

These essays have been published to prod the "slumbering giant," to arouse interest, and with God's blessing, to galvanize people to study and action.

This first essay, exploring the biblical perspective in education, deals with three clusters of questions.

I. What is the crisis in so-called "public" education today? Is it real, imagined or what?

II. How should the Body of Christ respond to the present situation? What do the Scriptures say about nurture? What contours do we give to a biblically-attuned educational confession in the 1970's?

III. What are the concerns of a Christian school — a school directed by the Word of God? What kind of teaching, learning and curriculum are required in a Christian school?

Let us begin with the present situation. Is it as bad as Silberman, Holt,[2] Friedenberg, and other critics fear? Certainly on the surface it is not. When we hear what our children are doing at school, when we visit the school we can hardly hold back the wish that we could go to school all over again. Teachers and pupils are often literally deluged by mountains of learning paraphernalia — undreamed of only a few short years ago.

Yet, despite such educational wealth, it is becoming distressingly clear that all the educational glitter is not gold. And we are only fooling ourselves if we imagine it is. Indeed, our children are blessed with unparalleled opportunities to learn, our teachers have the best ever in learning materials, our schools are generally functional and beautiful. No doubt we have individual teachers and schools which are exceptions. Yet to our horror we are discovering that we have raised a generation without vision, without commitment, without meaning and purpose in life. Many parents have given their children the best in education only to realize that the children are not interested; in fact, the children often reject everything their parents stand for and believe in.

Here we are close to the heart of the problem and it is just at this juncture that Christians can further the analysis. Educational failure simply reflects the root crisis in the American way of life.

The American way of life has been built on the melting pot idea.[3] Basic convictions are private, to be exercised on Sunday. During the week one must leave basic convictions at home, and work together with his neighbours for the common good. This is how the American experiment set out to maintain individual freedom and at the same time to meet societal demands.

The attempt has become embroiled in contradictions. Everyone is supposed to be free and equal based on the supposed commonness of Reason. However, freedom and equality have turned out to be ideas that oppose one another, even as they depend on one another. History has shown that if everyone is free, then not everyone is equal; in fact, it is necessary to curb anarchy by restricting the freedom of some. On the other hand, if everyone is equal in the sense of sameness, then there is a restriction of the freedom of everyone. Every man is levelled to the level of everyone else, and he is no longer free. Today it appears that one is only free if he is not equal, and only equal if he is not free.

This inherent tension in the American experiment — between individual freedom and societal demands, between free and equal — is reflected in the school system. For it was just the school which was chosen to be the instrument to educate its citizens in the American way of life. Horace Mann, the father of public schools in America, spoke in glorious terms of education bringing in the millenium of Christian hope. In fact, as Ivan Illich[4] has again called to our attention, the school has "become the established church of secular times." John Dewey, himself not without influence on American education, was also convinced that education was religion. Rousas Rushdoony has written a book in this vein entitled *The Messianic Character of American Education.*[5] Henry Steele Commager, the well-known historian, expresses it well: "From the first then education was the American religion. It was – and is – in education that we put our faith; it is our schools and colleges that are the peculiar objects of public largess and private benefaction; even in architecture we proclaim our devotion, building schools like cathedrals."[6]

Education is salvation; school is church; teachers are the new high priests; the scientific method or science is god. This is the vision which permeates the system of education in Canada and the United States. "It is," as one Canadian report expresses it, "a vision of greatness and dignity for the individual through the exercise of public and private responsibility."[7] The aim is that all men may "reach a new plateau of human commitment to the common good."

Individual Integrity Versus Societal Demands

"The democratic classroom is both the incubator and the cradle of democracy, and the teacher is its parent and guardian." Providing "learning experiences aiming at a thousand different destinies. . .at the same time [it strives] to educate toward a common heritage and common citizenship is the basic challenge" of our society.

To jar us into realizing just how unbiblical this educational spirit is, we will read the preface of a government report on education and then compare it with certain biblical passages.

"The underlying aim of education is to further man's unending search for truth. Once he possesses the means to truth all else is within his grasp. Wisdom and understanding, sensitivity, compassion, and responsibility, as well as intellectual honesty and personal integrity, will be his guides in adolescence and his companions in maturity. This is the message that must find its way into the minds and hearts of all children. This is the key to open all doors. It is the instrument which will break the shackles of ignorance, of doubt, and of frustration; that will take all who respond to its call out of their poverty, their slums and their despair; that will give mobility to the crippled; that will illuminate the dark world of the blind and bring the deaf into communion with the hearing. . .This above will be our task."

This paragraph is not just swollen language or the effusions of naive optimism. It is the statement of deep faith — faith in man, in his autonomy and ultimacy. Man must and can, if he will, control his destiny.

Now let us read Isaiah 35:4-6; (Also compare Isaiah 42:7 and Psalm 146.)

"Look, your God is coming,
vengeance is coming,
the retribution of God;
he is coming to save you!
Then the eyes of the blind shall be opened,
the ears of the deaf unsealed,
then the lame shall leap like a deer
and the tongues of the dumb sing for joy."

What the Scriptures confess to be the redeeming work of Christist He will open the eyes of the blind, unstop the ears of the deaf and give mobility to the crippled, etc. — the American system confesses to be the result of education. Missing the key to knowledge which is Christ, it is no wonder that man is lost in God's world. This is the real crisis in America.

Let us work out the matter in more detail. The problems intensify because, in accord with the American way of being free and equal, society attempts to fulfill both individual and societal needs in *one* public school system. The democratic community, to be sure, wishes to respect the individual's identity, dignity and integrity — his uniqueness. But since stressing individual uniqueness tends to divide the nation, the democratic classroom must accentuate whatever is held in common by all. It must establish the necessary bonds and common ground between individual students.

In our society criminals are imprisoned, and the mentally ill are confined to special institutions. And, in order that our children will not have deviant views and cause trouble, they are put in school where they are cut to specifications, neatly packaged, inspected and then certified. We can now rest confident that they will toe the line and play the American game. The school becomes a least-common-denominator institution which neither really serves the community well nor respects individual convictions. The important matters in life can really only be hinted at because it is these matters about which there are deep differences of opinion. The school tends to concentrate, inasmuch as that is possible, on the non-debatable. When key issues are touched upon, as they must be, attempts are made to be non-controversial by presenting all the various viewpoints. Since the student is to decide by himself which option to choose, he soon gets the idea that it does not really matter too much one way or the other.

Both students and teachers must leave their basic beliefs at home because they may offend others. Teachers in such public classrooms face untold problems. They must not upset the American applecart by giving away to their students their beliefs about the basic issues in life. At least they may only express what is in agreement with the party line; only that which, it is said, offends none. Teachers are only to present *the facts,* that is, what the ruling elite, the WASP, declare to be the facts.

As a result there can be no presentations of life-giving perspectives which will inspire the students and give them a framework in which to mature. This is serious business;

the more so since the teacher is the secular preacher in modern society. If he gives no vision or direction, who does? The end result is a lack of commitment and therefore a lack of meaning in life.

In this context — and that is being emphasized today — the best that can be done is to stress the need for commitment, for purpose in life, and for a concern with ideas and values — without further elaboration. To elaborate further and to give content in any instance would offend certain segments of the populace which are committed to opposing viewpoints. The supposed way out of this delimma is to mouth all the phrases about the importance of values, etc., but to leave them all contentless. In actual fact, short of complete nihilism, it is impossible to leave them completely contentless. However, insofar as they are given content, there is a lack of tolerance and a beginning of discrimination.

The antinomies, confusions and ambiguities such a policy causes in education are strikingly clear, for example, in so-called sex education.[8] Since differing faith communities have differing conceptions of the nature of marriage, the state school has to leave open the question of the real nature of marriage. If it taught any one view it would be discriminating against those holding divergent views. But it must teach something. Consequently, in least-common-denominator fashion, under the guise of factuality and neutrality, the school teaches only the mechanics and techniques of sex. By default students are taught that sex is more or less all there is to marriage. The Christian view of marriage — that it is basically a relationship of fidelity, troth or love between husband and wife for life based on sexual union — cannot be taught.

The situation is ridiculous but true. In order to avoid discrimination and in the name of tolerance a least-common-denominator view of marriage is taught which discriminates just as much and is actually just as intolerant as any other view.

While being urged in this way to commit themselves to democracy as a way of life, students are in fact encouraged to postpone, as long as possible, decisions on the major issues of life. "I reserve the right to suspend judgment" – that is the Western way of life. It is the religion of commitment to non-commitment. And it is this religion which today is shaken at its roots. It is just this right to suspend judgment, considered as American as cherry pie, which has given rise to the uncommitted generation. We have, much to our chagrin, discovered that productivity, not liberty, has been our focus; consensus, not dignity, our concern. Our supposed stability has been unmasked – and none too gently – as only lack of surface disturbances. Today's crisis is one of the spirit. It is not only that we can no longer believe in ourselves or that we no longer believe in God. It almost seems that we have lost the capacity to believe in anything. We are disillusioned, lost and alone.

In this context it is perhaps well to take note of one argument often used, even by Christians, against the establishment of Christian schools. We must not, it is said, force our children to become Christians; they must be free to choose. They must take in the facts and then, reaching the age of discretion, decide for themselves. This argument, whether its proponents are fully aware of it or not, is fully in line with the suspend-judgment view of the American way. The irony involved is tragic. Parents fail to give leadership in regard to the most important questions in life, even as they consider it essential that they help Johnny learn how to dress, how to use money, and how to eat. They know it would be an abdication of their responsibility to leave their children without guidance in these areas. They would be virtually giving their children up to destruction. But that is just what such parents are doing in regard to the major questions in life. Such parents

James H. Olthuis

should not be surprised that we are burdened with the uncommitted generation. What one sows he also reaps. Christians should be especially aware of this: "Train up a child in the way that he shall go and when he is old he will not depart from it."

II. The Biblical Witness

Indeed, we are now ready to ask what the Scriptures have to say about education. The Scriptures are emphatic that parents must nurture their children in the fear and admonition of the Lord. Let the children come to me, says Christ. Fathers, don't make your children angry beyond measure, but nourish them fully in the nurture and mind of the Lord. (Eph. 6:4; Matt. 19:14; Mark 10:4; Luke 18:16)

At the same time the Scriptures make clear that the mandate to obey parents and the charge to lead children is only valid within the context of the Kingdom of God. Children obey because they are hearing the Word of God from their parents, not simply because father says so. God established the covenant with Abraham, the father of all believers. The sermon of Moses directs all of Israel, not only parents, to teach the children when they are standing and when they are lying. (Deut. 6:4)

The entire Body of Christ is mandated to nurture its younger members in the fear of the Lord. At first this nurture was almost exclusively parental — the parents led the child's development in every aspect. But as the child grew, others also shared in leading. And as history unfolded and life became more complex it was evident that the parents simply could not lead in every area. Nations found it necessary to call up their young sons for military training. Soon the specialized tasks which developed could only be taught in special trade schools. And gradually it became clearer that more general schools were necessary in order to help sharpen, develop and deepen a child's analytic powers of discernment. Thus the school emerged with its own distinct structures as an instructional formative community of teachers and pupils. Its specific task is to form the student's power to discern and thus make it possible to better form himself and society.

Parental education is still very real and most important, but it is different than and distinct from school education. We will develop this further in a moment. The point here is that whatever the education, it must bring up children in the fear of the Lord.

When we begin from the biblical perspective and return to our present situation, it is abundantly clear that in order to lead students to a knowledge of their calling in the world as witnesses of the King, not only is a home based in the Scriptures necessary, but a school is necessary in which the name of Jesus Christ is openly and continually confessed as the only name given under heaven whereby one can be saved. The education must be Spirit-infused, Christ-centred and God-honoring. It must be education in the only Name – not in the name of science, freedom, democracy, or even humanity. The Body of Christ must, as never before, unite and confess that Christ is Lord in school education. Further mandated to work out our salvation with fear and trembling, Christians must strive for a more specific articulation of their basic commitment, one that is specially geared for and relevant to education. This confession, when fleshed out, could serve as the framework for a white paper which we could present to the nation – and thus call it back to Christ as the Way, the Truth, and the Life.

Needed: An Educational Confession

In the complexity of contemporary civilization we

require such an educational confession. And this confession ought to be given a measure of clarity in terms of a written statement of principle, or educational creed, so that Christians may reflect and act together in the educational area of life, and so that the world may know the direction and goal of our Christian way of living. Such a written confession would act as a channel between the Scriptures and the life of today. It could serve as a basis for action, as an ideal to realize, and as a call to others to join in a common confession and a common walk in joyful obedience to the one Lord.[9]

In saying this we do not want to minimize the importance of ecclesiastical confessions. But we do want to stress the need for worked-out confessions in areas beyond the institutional church. Taking into consideration the historical situation, it is well to examine for a moment the relation between church creeds and educational creeds.

The confessions of a (denominational) institutional church should not take the place of a Christian educational confession since a school is a school and an institutional church is an institutional church. Each of these structures requires a confession relevant to that structure, though in each instance that confession will be a response to the Scriptures. To act as if a church creed can be a school creed is to confuse and mislead. For one is then readily given the false idea that schools can only be of a Christian character in an indirect manner, namely through the institutional church and its creeds. In this way the institutional church is somehow identified with the entire range of the Kingdom of God so that all non-ecclesiastical organizations must to a lesser or greater degree be subject to and dependent on the church if they are to maintain a Christian character. The result of this approach in effect is the establishment of church schools. Moreover, to employ church creeds as school creeds is to take the easy way out in a difficult situation — as if our spiritual fathers had worked it all out correctly and in detail for later centuries and for later developments. It is to take the way of fear — as if the Spirit no longer leads His people so that they grow in the grace and knowledge of Jesus Christ attuned to His Word. Actually, it may be the way of little faith — refusing to heed the admonition to work out our own salvation with fear and trembling, for it is the Lord Who is working in us. (Phil. 2:12f)

The creeds of the institutional church were not intended to be and should not be looked upon as school creeds. They were written at a time when schools as we envision them today had not yet developed. They do not *specifically* express the directives of the Word of God for an educational enterprise and thus do not deal with modern educational problems and current anti-Christian views of the schooling process.

The church creeds are more general and wider in scope than the educational creed. They make the confession of Christians for all of life — thus also for school. But they speak the central, basic, concentrated language characteristic of a community at worship, a language which holds equally for all areas of life. The educational particularization is not yet worked out. An educational creed is more limited, yet in its restriction it is able to provide a more complete and more exact spelling out of the demands of the Word for education.

In this way an educational creed in no way replaces or competes with the church creeds. Rather, they complement each other. Rather than undermining or taking away from the integral confession of the Body of Christ, an educational creed deepens and enriches that confession. At a fundamental level there is a unity to our confession, the unity found in the Word of God as the norm for all confessing.

James H. Olthuis

Needed: Christian Schools

But not only must the mind of Christ be confessed to be the only way in social studies, reading, history, physics, and all the other subjects, but education itself in which concerted efforts are made to walk on this way in the entire curriculum, is needed. Christian education today means, concretely, a Christian school. Such a school is supported by the Body of Christ at large, organized into a school society. With the cooperation and support of the members by means of the school board which oversees the religious direction of the school, a team of teachers are free to fulfill their teaching office and open up children to the wonders of the creation in the light of the Scriptures.

Christian schools are for proclaiming the vision of the Kingdom in the schoolish way of teaching. Schools herald the good tidings in the way of schools rather than churches. Basically a Christian school is a channel in which God's grace flows to the healing of nations. Christian schools aim at training children, young people, and finally young adults to take their place in society as Christians. And because, in God's grace, Christians have been put in the proper place from which they can properly see relations, structures and patterns in the world around them, such education and such informed and guided young people work for the blessing of the nation at large. Christian schools are frontier posts in the battle against the power of humanism. Such schools are not antiseptic isolation booths, insulating the pupils from the big, bad world. They are not game preserves where together we hide our heads ostrich-like in the sand. Even if we wanted such hotbeds, they are impossibilities. Sin cannot be walled out. Teachers, pupils and curriculum are still in need of daily conversion.

Schools, according to the Word, in the Spirit, are like

huddles before the football game. Huddles are only part of the game, yet it is the part of the game in which one gets direction for further play. Without such clear direction, without gathering in huddles, everyone is confused and in each other's hair. Schools are the huddles which enable students to continue to learn, as they have learned in the family, the way that they must walk in life.

One of the real difficulties about the Christian witness in the world today is its lack of unity. One of the causes of this lack of unity is simply that our children have been educated *not* in the way of the Lord. Today, since there are few Christian schools, some Christians think that in the game of life we're playing baseball, others think we're playing football, some are playing ping-pong, some are doing handstands, some are canoeing. Only when Christians unitedly begin to play as they ought – as *one* body – will their witness be of *one* piece in the world.

It is important to note at this point that although the Scriptures do not explicitly mention schools as we know them – for the simple reason that such schools did not exist in biblical times – it does not mean that Christian schools lack foundation in the Scriptures. For not only do we have the explicit command that we are to educate our children in the fear of the Lord, we also know that God created the world by His Word; that without His Word nothing was made. That certainly includes schools. We have the assurance of faith that there is a Word of God for the school. The whole area of education is an area which is responsive to the Word of God. Thus, it is also contrary to the Scriptures, in the fashion of some, to talk about the school as a human institution over against divine institutions such as the church or marriage. It is true that man develops schools, but so does he set up churches and enter into marriages. The very possibility of setting up churches, entering into marriage, and establishing schools is only possible because of the Word of God. If a church is

James H. Olthuis

to be Christian, if a family is to be Christian, and if a school is to be Christian, there is the further demand that one set up these various communities inspired by the Spirit in heartfelt obedience to the Lord.

Indeed, to recognize each thing after its own kind; state as state, church as church, school as school, family as family, and so forth, is to honor the different ways God has ordered society. Doing justice to living in the Spirit and walking the Way of the Word today means also to do justice to the Word in its multi-dimensional character and to the concomitant multiplicity of the paths which all point in the same Way. There is *one* Word of the Lord and there is *one* Way in accordance with this Word. At the same time the Scriptures point out that this one Word is a multiplicity of words structuring the various areas of life, and that correspondingly the *one* Way is composed of a network of ways in obedience to the words which are the Word of God.

III. The Christian School

Now what is the Word of God for the school? What is the structure and nature of schooling? Clearly this demands much communal struggle and reflection in order to biblically determine these central matters in connection with the school. To outline some of the matters which will be dealt with in later chapters, I will comment briefly on three important areas.

The educational curriculum
The teaching/learning process
The child in the school

The Educational Curriculum

Since a school is to open up to its students the wonders of creation, it is of paramount importance for a

Christian school that it take seriously the biblical confession that the Word structures and directs the creation until this day. If one limits the Word of God to the Scriptures, the best he can have is a school with a Bible. Without this confession, except for Bible class, prayer and an occasional song, a Christian school would be the same as any other school. The Scriptures, of course, are necessary. Without the Scriptures as the Word of God our eyes cannot be opened to the Word of God which holds for creation. Without the Scriptures we cannot know Jesus Christ. However, the Scriptures lose their full impact if they alone are considered the Word of God. In fact, it is directly contrary to the testimony of the Scriptures themselves.[10]

However, if we grow in the awareness that God's Word structures creation in all its activities, and that in Christ, according to the Scriptures, we have the key to this Word and thus to creation, unlimited vistas open up before our eyes. Everywhere God surrounds us by His Word and calls for obedience. Everywhere He calls us to preach this Gospel to every creature and to teach them to take up their task as gardeners in creation. (Matt. 28 and Gen. 2)

In school this learning takes place by means of a curriculum. The educational curriculum is the unifying framework which ties the teaching staff, the students, and the subject matter together in the setting of the school. While parents have the responsibility for determining the spiritual direction of their children's education, the body of educators in the Christian community has the office of articulating the content of the educational curriculum. The curriculum leads the students through the various aspects of creation so that the student learns that God's Word holds everywhere, and so that he learns to responsibly submit to the Lord. Without such a curriculum, a Christian school is simply not living up to its calling. One of the needs of the hour is a more expansive and more developed biblically-attuned curriculum. One could say that a school curriculum is a course of studies in which pupils are led through the various areas or rooms of the creation while they remain in the school room. This does not mean, of course, that education must always happen in the same place. The students can be taken to a factory. But the fact of the matter is that even when they are at a factory, they are not there for the purposes of the factory, but they are there to learn about what is going on in the factory. Even there they are doing it in the nature and the way of the school.

The fact that a Christian school will have a curriculum built on the idea that there is a creation ordered by the powerful Word of God, sets off the biblical view in a Christian school clearly from both the classical approach and from the current child-centered approach. The classical approach reduces the order of creation and the Word for creation to something rational. At the same time the child-centred approach sees man as the autonomous actor who must give structure to the chaotic creation. The principial difference between the biblical approach and these two other approaches cannot be overestimated, certainly not in the context of a school.

In the classical approach the teacher and the subject matter taught were the centre of the classroom. The teacher had the truth and the authority. Her concern was to transport this logically conceived truth into the minds of the students. The school was a dispensary of facts, with each pupil considered to be the same size and shape pill bottle. If a pupil gathered in twenty percent of the facts (the bottle is one-fifth full), he flunked; if the bottle is eighty per cent full, he passed with flying colours. Little consideration was given to the individual makeup and needs of the students. Each student was judged solely by his ability or inability to assimilate facts in a logically precise manner.

At the same time, since education takes place within the structures of creation, a Christian view of education rejects the child-centred approach. In this tradition creation is considered a chaos without order; man is heralded as the creator rather than unfolder of order and meaning. Here the emphasis is on the student's individuality, responsibility and freedom. The *search* for truth rather than truth itself is the concern; knowledge is only knowledge when it is discovered, apprehended, interpreted and used by pupils. Ideally, the pupil should make his own choice of content under the guidance of the teacher. Attempting to allow a child's spontaneity and inquisitiveness free play, and at the same time well aware that it would be confusing to send him on voyages of discovery without charts of some sort, proponents of this approach face fundamental problems, problems which, I should add, can never be adequately resolved when the needs and interests of the individual child are elevated to the place of the norm.

However, in spite of its praiseworthy concern for the student or individual, the contemporary child-centred approach is no more biblical than the older curriculum-centred practice. And although it is wrong to consider the teacher's authority an end in itself, it is just as wrong in the fashion of the child-centred way to consider the freedom of an individual (whether young or old) to be, in principle, absolute and uncurtailed.

The Teaching Office

The Body of Christ is called upon to subdue and develop the earth by, among other things, guiding students into a deeper understanding of God's world and its history. Through the execution of this teaching office in the school, pupils and students are to attain cultural maturity grounded in the biblical faith so that they can take up their specific responsibilities and vocations in a manner pleasing to the Lord. The knowledge that schools too are responses to the Word of God and that they have a specific character, is most important. It means that biblically-normed school education demands more than a simple confession of Christ on the part of individual teachers. Simply because one is a Christian does not qualify him to be a teacher, just as the fact of being in Christ does not qualify one to be a plumber. Christians too, in Christ, are to work out their salvation with fear and trembling. Some members of the Body of Christ have been given the task of working out their salvation with fear and trembling in the area of education. These people have been given a calling, a gift, an office – the office of teaching. According to, and in conformity with, Ephesians 4, in these latter days the Body of Christ has been given many gifts, and one of them is teaching.

Today, the task of nurture is too complex and too difficult for parents alone; teachers – educational teachers – are called to office so that our children can be prepared through general education to stand firm and not be tossed to and fro with every wind of doctrine.

Teaching is a free and responsible activity. Such teaching should take place in concert so that the students feel and know that all the teachers are working together and that there is one direction to the school and there are concrete ways in which the curriculum shows this one direction. Teachers are directly and communally responsible to the Lord for the execution of the educational task. This responsible freedom must be protected against any constraint or domination of the state, the industrial complex, the church, or other societal structures. The biblical view of service (or *diakonia*) means neither that the authority of the teaching office is ultimate and final, nor that the freedom of the pupil is ultimate or final. Rather, the biblical concept of service means that the authority of the teaching office is for the sake of the freedom of the pupil. This view is uniquely Christian. It means that if one has the insight, he has the authority to demand respect for his office. But he also has the insight to realize that his authority is not his own. It is an authority which comes from the understanding that his office is to provide the freedom for those under him so that they too can responsibly go about their task. Educated so that students can see the meaningfulness of the Christian life, as God's representatives, students are thus faced with the responsibility of choosing to assume their calling in the unfolding of creation and the coming of the Kingdom. (II Cor. 5:19, 20)

The Pupil in the Classroom

The student as an image-bearer of the Lord is a whole person to be guided at school toward responsible maturity in preparing for his calling in the unfolding of creation and the coming of the Kingdom of God. The child in his heart must respond to the Word of the Lord. This means that we are utterly opposed to the older theory which considers man to be basically a rational, moral being, and at the same time we reject the modern theories which reduce man to a biological organism which has developed a facade of personality. A Christian view of the child in the educational setting rejects the classical curriculum-centred approach since it tends to reduce students to the status of intellectual absorbers of information without paying heed to the individuality of the child.

At this juncture it is important for Christian education to realize that it must do justice to the basic nature of the student as a fellow image-bearer of God. Children are people. As people students may never be treated as objects to be manipulated or brainwashed. The student is always a person, a unique subject called by his Creator to make his own response. This being the case, one cannot really decide for a person, he can only lead him to decide. One ought not teach subjective responses, values and virtues, and thus attempt to make a person be good. Rather, the emphasis must be on teaching the norm in motivating the student to want to make the right response from his heart. It is wrong to attempt behaviouristically to condition a child to go through certain motions without teaching him responsibility so that he will understand their necessity. No doubt one can get a child to do as he pleases, but unless he wants to do these things from the heart, nothing has really been gained. A teacher may only formatively address himself to one or many aspects of the child's life. In so doing, he permits the child the freedom to relate the nurture to his life as a whole and in so doing he safeguards the freedom of the child to respond from the heart and in the process form himself. Nurture or education which is not pedagogical, that is, nurture which does not foster growing independence and responsibility on the part of pupils, is anti-normative. One cannot teach a child to be good; he can only be motivated to want to be good.

In this context one more matter deserves our attention. Often in Christian circles we are told, and even more often in practice it becomes clear, that a belief in the total depravity of the child dictates discipline in the sense of negativity; a holding-down of evil in the child. This idea of biblical discipline does not correspond with the Scriptures. Biblical discipline does not mean negative restricting, but a positive guiding of the child in his desire to learn. Within the idea of negative discipline lies a serious misunderstanding and misuse of the scriptural teaching. Man is indeed totally depraved. He is lost in sin except the Spirit of God renew him. Scripture is emphatic on this point and no one must have any illusions or attempt to meddle with this teaching. The direction, the pattern, the fabric of a person's life outside of Christ is anti-God.

However, that does not mean that man is unable on certain functional levels to seek and to do the right. Outside of Christ a man is still a man, even though he is on the wrong road and he is in danger of losing his very existence as a man. By virtue of the fact that he is still man, he desires on the functional level to do things right. Everyone wants to learn, to speak properly, to be fair, to build correctly, to drive safely, to be faithful, and so forth. Everyone has such desires because the structure of his manhood is held in place by the Word of God. That means that the existence of such desires is no evidence of the fact, as has often been suggested, that man is basically good at heart. No, the existence of such desires only speaks of the goodness of the Word of God calling man to response and holding man in existence. Indeed, the tragedy involved is that outside of Christ, man's evil heart works out this learning, this speaking, this building, this driving safely in a way which is alien to the Word of God; the way of death. All that I am saying is what all of us know and experience every day: outside of Christ man can still build homes which are homes. They can still have relationships with other people that stop short of murder; they still have some awareness of justice; they still help each other, etc. If these things were not so, then it would be impossible for Christians to exist in the world. Neither would there be a possibility for an unbeliever to do anything.

This means that these built-in human desires must be appealed to in education. They must be stimulated, guided and formed. They must be nurtured if learning is to take place. They must be unfolded in a certain way so that the child begins to form himself in a way which is well pleasing to the Lord. The Scriptures too give many examples of this kind of perspective. Psalm 127 exclaims: "Except the Lord build the house they labour in vain who build." Man can build houses, in many respects *good* houses, whether aesthetically, technically, economically, etc. But in the end such homes are vanity, nothing, if they are not openly confessed to have been in the power of the Lord, and in the direction of obedience.

In summary, let me say that the total depravity of our children — which we share with them — may not be used as an excuse to deprive them of the pleasures of learning in a positive, alive, motivated environment.

The lostness of mankind in sin does ~~not~~ mean that if a person does not put his trust in the Lord the learning which he does will be, finally, of no avail.

A Call to Concerted Christian Action

There is a crisis in education today. Everywhere people are perishing for lack of vision. And everywhere voices are raised offering solutions to the crisis. Only the Christians seem to be sleeping. Christians, mandated to lead their children to find their place in God's Kingdom, seem unconcerned that this leading does not take place in the public school. The Christian family and church pull one way; the school pulls another. And there is nothing in the wind which promises anything better. The only hope is that those who confess Christ's name in the world will squarely face the issue of the biblical mandate to establish Christian schools. It is sad but striking that although everyone squirms when he must go under the knife and submit to an operation, so many Christians appear to unblinkingly offer their children up to the educational knife operating on their children. We continue to offer up our children to the modern Molochs of education with nary a sound, and our children are getting burnt. Or to change the metaphor in accordance with Ephesians 4, right now many of our children, and many of our neighbour's children, are being tossed to and fro by every wind of doctrine. They are at the mercy of every evil man practicing his particular deceit, and we do nothing about it. And those of us who have established Christian schools are not really acting as good Samaritans. We allow our fellow Christians to go on without really offering the help of the Christian community. We would rather pass by than have to face the task, the challenge of working together with other Christians on the cause of Christian education. After all, these people have other ethnic backgrounds, they have other traditions; it is far easier to let them go. Is that being a good Samaritan? Are we facing the issue squarely?

People are funny, one might say — passing strange. They generally will do everything for their children; they often do too much. But what they can do for them with effort, and what they ought to do with dedication, they often do not do. "Can a woman forget her sucking child that she should not have compassion on the son of her womb?" (Isaiah 49) In most cases, no. But many of us and many of our neighbours are so brainwashed or so blind that we do forget our children at this point. Don't be fooled by the fact that a child does not overnight reject the vision of the Kingdom. For surely he is learning when he goes to school, and he is being taught to put his life to work in the service of some cause or purpose, including non-commitment to anything.

If we continue to allow our children to be taught in schools which at best ignore the Lord; if we do not continue to improve our schools, do we not fall under the indictment of the Lord just as much as when we neglect to speak of him in our homes?

Christ's warning is to the point here: "Whoever receives one such child in my name receives me. But if a man is a cause of stumbling to one of these little ones who have faith in me, it would be better for him to have a millstone hung around his neck and be drowned in the depths of the sea." (Matt. 18:5, 6)

There is not a moment to lose. All confessors of Christ must join hands and see to it that the Lord's name is praised in education.

James H. Olthuis

Footnotes

[1]Charles Silberman, *Crisis in the Classroom* (New York: Random House, 1970), p. 12. Please note: other quotations cited in the essay are found on pp. 10, 14, 19, 20, 22, 28.

[2]For example, E. Friedenberg, *The Vanishing Adolescent* (New York: Beacon Press, 1959) and *Coming of Age in America* (New York: Random House, 1965); J. Herndon, *The Way it Spozed to Be* (New York: Simon and Schuster, 1968) and *The Way You're Spozed to Teach* (New York: Simon and Schuster, 1972); John Holt, *How Children Fail* (New York: Dell, 1970) and *What Do I Do Monday?* (New York: Dell, 1972); H. Kohl, *36 Children* (New York: Norton, 1967).

[3]Although Canada, with some justification, prides itself on being a social "mosaic" which recognizes and encourages differences rather than enforcing a "melting pot" ideal which leads to a bland, homogenized uniformity, this country still (with Quebec as an exception?) operates on the assumption that every Canadian at bottom agrees on the spiritual direction which life should take. For that reason the same basic pattern emerges as in the United States.

[4]Ivan Illich, *Celebration of Awareness: A Call to Institutional Reform* (New York: Harper and Row, 1969), p. 127.

[5]Rousas Rushdoony, *The Messianic Character of American Education* (Philadelphia: Craig Press, 1963).

[6]Henry Steele Commager, "Free Public Schools – A Key to National Unity" in *Crucial Issues in Education* (New York: Holt, Rinehart, and Winston, 1969), p. 7.

[7]*Living and Learning*. The Report of the Provincial Committee on Aims and Objectives of Education in the Schools of Ontario (Ontario Department of Education: Toronto, 1968), p. 6. Also compare pp. 9, 121, 21.

[8]Instead of dividing the Christian community, the "sex" issue should galvanize us into concerted action in support of Christian schools where the biblical view of marriage and family could be taught freely.

[9]In an appendix to this essay located at the back of the book, a

first working out of such a creed is presented for communal use and discussion.

[10]For a treatment of the biblical testimony, see Bernard Zylstra's "Thy Word Our Life" in *Will all the King's men. . .* by James H. Olthuis, et. al (Toronto: Wedge Publishing Foundation, 1972), p. 153.

2

THE HISTORY OF EDUCATION
WITH PARTICULAR EMPHASIS
ON CHRISTIAN EDUCATION

The Struggle for Christian Education in Western History

by John C. VanderStelt

Children of the Lord cannot accept educational theories and practices which dishonor God's Name and violate the true meaning of education and the rest of life.

In this essay we will trace the main educational developments from out of the past into the present. Because we are limited by space, we shall have to be highly selective.

First, it is not history but the *Word* of the Lord that is our basic norm. This Word of God holds true for everything. It also holds true for the historical development of education.

Second, as Christians we may not ignore *history*. To be familiar with our historical background is not a luxury but a necessity. Our life today is determined in many respects by the structural development and religious struggle within our historical past. We are mainly interested here in the history of *education*. We wish to discover how in this crucial area of cultural power people have acquitted themselves of their educational calling in obedience or in disobedience to the Word of the Lord.

Our point of departure for this brief survey will be that period in history when education ceased to be mere training at home and in the field, shop, and army, and became more or less "formal," that is, a formal training of pupils by professional educators on elementary, secondary and advanced levels.

A quick way of getting at the essence of education in general is to concentrate on the nature of *advanced* education; that is, upon these centres or institutions where one theorizes about principles, discusses and formulates various ideas, develops new insights, and passes on to others the results of investigations. What is learned and taught in such educational centres becomes sooner or later the content of the curriculum in other and more elementary institutions of formal learning. Once we know what educators have been cooking up in the kitchens of higher learning, we have a good idea of what thousands and even millions of students have been spoon-fed in the cafeterias of primary and secondary schools throughout the history of the Western world.

Education in the Greek and Roman World

1. Religious Nature of Greek and Roman Education

The pagan Greeks and Romans did not know the Creator. Neither did they know the Word of the Lord. Nor did they understand the real nature of man and the true meaning of life and society. Nevertheless, they, too, were human creatures, and by virtue of this they could not escape being deeply religious in all their activities, including the educational ones.

Poets, musicians, mathematicians, rhetoricians, and philosophers provided in various ways the cultural leadership, particularly with respect to the training of young men who wanted to become the leaders of the future. Sophists — "wise men" — travelled as itinerant teachers from one cultural centre to the next. Philosophers — "lovers of wisdom" — usually settled down in one or two centres of cultural power. All sorts of educators vied with one another for the privilege of giving formal instruction to those free citizens who could afford the luxury of advanced education in return for financial remuneration.

The instruction that was given consisted primarily of discussing such fundamental questions as: What does it mean to be human? What is the value of life? What is the nature and goal of society? What reforms are needed? What is the ultimate aim of all culture?

Try to imagine for a moment having to answer these and other related basic questions of life *without* the Light of God's Word and Spirit in your heart! If the Word of the Lord is not the cornerstone of life in general and the capstone of education in particular, what then is education? How could the Greeks and Romans answer such questions? What was the solution? *What* did they teach?

2. Education and the *polis* (City-State)

From the fifth century before Christ until the end of the fourth century after Christ, it was a common belief that true or meaningful education was determined ultimately by the idea of a political community; that is, the *polis* or city-state. It was the city-state that bound life together and gave meaning to what parents, workers, tradesmen, and soldiers did. The *polis* constituted the perfect society. This all-encompassing political institution determined the essence of true humanity. The *polis* was the most perfect realization of all cultural ideals. It also directed and structured all educational aims and activities.

In his classic three-volume study of ancient education, *Paideia: Ideals of Greek Culture,* Werner Jaeger writes that:

> Greek culture first assumed its classical form in the polis or city-state...The polis is the focus of Greek history in the

John C. VanderStelt

> classical era, the most important period of the nation's development, and is therefore the centre of historical interest. . .to describe the Greek polis is to describe the whole Greek life. (Vol. I, pp. 77-78)

Individual persons might die but the political community continued to exist forever. Immortality came to mean being remembered by the city-state after one had died. The *polis* inspired all its citizens. The Greek idea of education cannot be understood properly apart from this all-embodying community idea.

Not knowing God and His Word, the Greeks and later on the Romans were unable to place things of life in their correct perspective. The framework of reference was not the scriptural Covenant and Kingdom but rather the city-state. The ideas and laws established by the philosophers and protected by the military formed the real content of education. Education was the process by means of which a person was converted (!) and made desirous to find his identity or selfhood in some form of political community.

The central thrust of this Greek understanding of life, culture, education, and teaching has made a great impact upon the subsequent history of Western civilization. Our Western world is still caught deep down in the grip of the Greek and Roman idea of the nature of education, the role of schools, the task of teachers, the purpose of formal education, and the structure of the curriculum. Professor Jaeger also writes in *Paideia* that:

> The polis is the sum of all its citizens and of all the aspects of their lives. It gives each citizen much, but it can demand all in return. Relentless and powerful, it imposes its way of life on each individual, and marks him for its own. From it are derived all the norms which govern the life of its citizens. Conduct that injures it is bad, conduct that helps it is good. . .both he [Plato] and Aristotle claim that all education should, in the perfect state, bear the imprint of the spirit of the state. . .To establish a legal standard by written law was for the Greeks an educational act. (I, 109)

48

> Law is the mother of philosophy...[Lawmakers are] the educators of their people...[Law is] the soul of the city. (I, 110)
>
> The polis gives each individual his due place in its political cosmos, and thereby gives him, besides his private life, a sort of second life, his *bios politikos.* Now every citizen belongs to two orders of existence; and there is a sharp distinction in his life between what is *his own (idion)* and what is communal *(koinon).* (I, 111)

3. The Structure of Society

Classical Greeks claimed that basically there were only three classes in society and that there were only four virtues (or norms). Each one of the classes had its own specific virtue or norm. The three classes in society were the following:

a. The class of *rulers* or leaders who had to obey the virtue of being godly or *wise;* that is, philosophically knowledgeable.

b. The class of soldiers or *guards* who sought to be characterized by the virtue of *courage.* (For instance, heroes in battle became immortal.)

c. The class of *workers* at the bottom of the societal hierarchy. This class was comprised of shopkeepers, tradesmen, farmers, shepherds, builders, etc. This lower working class was to be motivated especially by the virtue of *prudence* and thus had to show self-control.

There was no specific class in society for the fourth virtue, namely *justice* or righteousness. The reason for this is that justice had to be seen in connection with the mutual relationships between the three above mentioned classes. It qualified society as a whole. Justice cemented or bound together the three classes with their respective virtues into the perfect community. Righteousness ensured that the members of each class in society performed their function as perfectly as possible. In the cosmos of the Greek city-state, the laws and justice became the central focus of living. So it becomes understandable why the constitution of the state was believed to be "the ideal educational system," and why "the problem of education was ultimately the problem of finding an absolute standard for human behavior." (I, 84) The lawgiver is the wise leader and the educator. Jaeger comments in this connection that "We must take education to mean the teaching of *arete* (virtue), which begins in childhood, and makes us wish to become perfect citizens, knowing how to command and to obey in accordance with law." (III, 224)

Knowledge, culture, politics, education, teacher, pupil, lawgiver, and citizen – all of these were inseparably related to one another. The one could not be defined and properly understood without the other. This peculiar world and life view with its attendant vision of education remained one of the fundamental assumptions in nearly all subsequent historically significant theories of education in our Western world.

4. Educational Method in the Ancient World

The perfect society was a righteous or harmonious society. Thus a person was perfect when he was a harmonious being. An educated person was one whose ethos and disposition has been formed in such a manner that as a mature citizen he would naturally fit into the ethos of the community at large.

To use a figure of speech taken from the world of agriculture, we can describe the entire educational process as follows: the good soil was the human nature of the student; the skillful farmer was the teacher who cultivated the young person in such a way that the latter became a mature being; the good seed was the instruction that was given and received; the watering of the tender plant was the educational process through which the young person learned to choose the right and hate the wrong; the tools to be used were the seven liberal arts or techniques by means of which the student was liberated and became a true human being. (The seven liberal arts were grammar, rhetoric, dialectic composing the *trivium,* and arithmetic, geometry, music, and astronomy composing the *quadrivium.*)

We have seen already that the real educators were the philosophers. The guide to the realm of the divine is knowledge. Only the philosophers possessed real knowledge. Through their theorizing they knew the truth. Philosophy was "the way to true power. . .the very centre of life. . .the saviour in time of need, because she possesses the solution to the most urgent of all social problems." (II, 264) Philosophers understood the nature of education and possessed the power to implement the purpose of it; namely, the *metanoia,* conversion, the turning around of the pupil or student, so that the latter too can enter into the kingdom of the *polis.*

A general consensus arose in Greece during the fourth century before Christ that all formal education should in essence be public, state education. This idea originated with the Greek philosophers who thought themselves to be the only and true interpreters of the meaning of life and society. It is basically for this ultimate purpose that they established schools of learning and instruction. Various intellectuals founded schools or colleges where they imparted their profound knowledge of the good life within the city-state. These first schools were of great historical significance for the future of all Western educational efforts.

The most important centres of advanced learning established by the philosophical educators of Greece were the Academy of Plato and the Lyceum of Aristotle in

51

John C. VanderStelt

Athens, the School of the Pythagoreans in southern Italy, the Centre of learning in Alexandria in northern Egypt, and the various schools of the Sophists who usually moved around from one place to another.

Later on this typically Greek view of education also became characteristic of the Roman theory and practice of education. As a matter of fact, it has continued to exist ever since that time until the present, notwithstanding the entrance of Christianity into the Eastern and Western world. Christianity did attempt up to a point to bend, modify, and redirect this essentially pagan educational philosophy, but it did not basically alter, reform, or restructure it in an inherently Christian manner.

The Ecclesiasticization of Greek and Roman Education by Christianity

During the period of the Old Testament, it was customary for the Israelites to teach children how to read and write at home. The priests and Levites assisted the parents with the instruction of children in the faith of the Covenant according to the Word of the Lord. Neither the state nor the philosophers were the ultimate sources of meaning. Israel had to learn to live by every word that proceeded from the mouth of the Lord God. Refusal to allow the God of heaven and earth to order their life was punished. The Babylonian captivity was such a punishment.

After Israel returned from its captivity in Babylon and at approximately the same time that advanced centres of learning were established in the Greek world, schools for formal training also began to be formed in Israel. These schools were located only in some of the main cities of the regained land of Israel. The primary aims of these educational centres were the training of leaders for temple service and biblical interpretation. Out of this rabbinical tradition arose the School of the Pharisees and the School of the Sadducees: the former thought strongly in terms of Israel as a politically distinct people; the latter were eager to compromise with the spirit of the Greek culture. The nature and result of the clash between these traditions of learning and what Christ taught as the Word-of-God-in-the-flesh; how the Pharisees and Sadducees joined the Romans and Greeks in common opposition to the Wisdom of God; and how Paul, formerly a Pharisee himself, came into conflict with the Greek mind when he was confronted by unbelieving philosophers on the Mount of Areopagus in Athens – all are too well known to need further elaboration at this point.

1. Christian Education Became *Church* Education

Approximately one century after Christ, Christians made serious attempts (for apologetic reasons) to incorporate some of the central ideas of the existing educational practices into their own Christian way of life. Werner Jaeger has sensed this very keenly. He wrote in his "Preface" to the second volume that "It was Greek paideia which laid the groundwork for the ardent, centuries-long competition between the Greek spirit and the Christian religion, each trying to master or assimilate the other, and for their final synthesis." (II, XI)

What occurred during the next two centuries has determined to a large extent the subsequent development of what has come to be known as "Christian education."

For various reasons some very influential Christian intellectual leaders began to advocate the idea that the Greek and Roman system of education could – without radical changes and harm – be included in and fused with their own Christian lifestyle. The only significant condition which had to be met was that all education should be made subservient to the teachings and goals of the established church. For this reason "Christian education" signified first of all ecclesiastical indoctrination in the Christian faith in accordance with the teachings of the Bible and the church fathers. Secondly, "Christian education" also meant the training of priests for the church and monks for the monasteries. Thirdly, it also implied that what the *polis* had been for the Greeks and Romans, now the *ecclesia* should be for the Christians. Finally, "Christian education" required that the theologian now take the place of the philosopher! The genuine educators who knew how to form cultured Christians were the theologians who were experts at employing the crowbars of pagan culture and learning, as provided by Greek and Roman philosophers, to pry open the fundamental meaning or truth of God's revealed Word. God was the great Pedagogue. Christ was the great Teacher. The Logos stood at the very core of all education and culture. In this manner the classical idea of education could be Christianized; that is, superseded, surpassed, and trumped, so it was thought.

Before long it became apparent, however, that the tools the Christians borrowed from the pagans turned out to be more than mere tools. There arose a blending, a mutual penetration and adaptation between classical education and Christianity. One of the first places where this occurred was in the Christian community of scholars at Alexandria in Egypt. It was here that "Greek Culture and the Christian Church were to be united in the mighty superstructure of Alexandrian Theology." (Werner Jaeger, *Early Christianity and Greek Paideia,* p. 90) Clement of Alexandria (150-217) and his pupil Origen (185-253) very deliberately sought to combine the two conflicting religions of the pagans and the Christians. These two men had a tremendous impact with their approach and views upon the leading educators in Asia Minor, especially Basil the Great (+ 330-397), Gregory Nazianzen (329-390), and

Gregory of Nyssa (+ 330-395). From Asia Minor this compromising mentality spread rather rapidly to the Christian world in the West, particularly to North Africa, Italy, France and England.

2. Christian Education Became *Public* Education.

At the end of the fourth century, emperor Theodosius ruled that Christianity (that is the church) from now on would be the official state religion (more accurately, the state *church*). This political development further ecclesiasticized the meaning of education. In fact, Christian education became essentially the educational system of ecclesiastical self-perpetuation and an affirmation of the supremacy of the state church over the rest of society and culture. Christian education became the means *par excellence* of training students so that when they were mature, educated, they would become loyal citizens, not of the *polis* in the earlier Greek and Roman sense of the word, but of the Christian state in the sense of the Holy Roman Empire with its seat and apex of power in the Church of Rome.

Closely connected with this was what was done with the seven liberal arts of Greek and Roman education. To these arts were *added* the study of theology, the three Christian virtues of faith, hope, and love (note that the four classical virtues of wisdom, courage, prudence, and justice were retained and complemented), and the investigation of ecclesiastical canon law. Theologians studied God and His revelation. They were the experts in explaining the Will of the Lord, providing wise (that is, godly) leadership, Christianizing the seven liberal arts. Theology became the queen of the sciences. The official church with its theology made education Christian. Without church and theology all education remained essentially non-Christian.

John C. VanderStelt

By virtue of the fact that the Roman Catholic Church dominated all of life as the official state religion, all so-called Christian education was "public" in nature and intent. It is wrong to close our eyes to the fact that the Roman Catholic Church did preserve and foster a culturally significant tradition of education which would otherwise have disappeared entirely during the often barbarous early Middle Ages. Nevertheless, the Christian community at that time erred in keeping all education subservient to the church. A church-controlled educational ideal has for centuries prevented scripturally directed Christian education from developing its own independent, distinctive manifestation. Though understandable, this kind of distorted development is not justifiable. Genuine, full-fledged Christian education remained suppressed by Church-controlled education by way of the Cathedral Schools of the bishops, the monastic centres of learning practised by various Orders within the Church, and other educational institutions which were established and operated by members of the church.

3. Christian Education in Disintegration

It is impossible to keep something suppressed for ever. That which is inherently unaffected by the redemption in Christ becomes sooner or later a serious threat to the very existence of the Christian religion. It had been the official teaching of the Church that in the classical world of nature and education a self-sufficient, natural light of reason was operative. The Church tried to embrace and keep in check this bundle of natural reason. Beginning during the thirteenth century, some of the leading centres of learning in the Western world started to throw off the ecclesiastical shackles. They tried to remove the churchly embrace and crawl out from underneath the umbrella of the non-academic Church institution. The natural light of reason strove to become more and more what it already was — self-sufficient and autonomous. It had resisted becoming Christianized all along. It had never wanted to be swallowed up in the theology and compromising attitude of established Christendom. What did not belong together, man had tried to unite in an artificial manner. What was known as "Christian education" during the Middle Ages carried within its own bosom the principial seed of its later disintegration.

Secularization of Education Since the Sixteenth Century

1. Modern variations and applications of classical education: all genuine education is "public"

From the cradle of new academic centres in Italy (cf. Salerno, Bologna, Padua and Florence), France (cf. Paris), and England (cf. Oxford and Cambridge) there arose, or was born, a new man. Man was his own law. Man possessed an inherent dignity and worth. Man was reborn; he was now the renaissance man. It was this spirit that took a hold of and swept through the studies of medicine, languages, ethics, philosophy, law, natural sciences and through the arts.

The wind of Humanism with its stress upon human dignity, swept along by the later storm of the religion of Reason, developed still later into the hurricane of the revolutionary spirit of the eighteenth-century Enlightenment. More and more educational theories and practices were intimately linked up with and fostered by the anti-Christian religion of human autonomy. One of the slogans of that era was: "Build schools. Tear down jails." It was believed that education delivers students and mankind in general from all evils and liberates them to inaugurate the utopian community of genuine toleration.

Teachers are the prophets, priests and kings. Schools and universities are the sacred temples. Man's own mind and heart is the source of revelation or meaning in life. The training of the rationalistic gentleman differs only in degree from the training of the political revolutionary.

Throughout the entire Western world this spirit of *religious* secularism took a hold eventually in all academic centres of advanced learning. It was intensified by the rise of Evolutionism, Historicism, Pragmatism, Positivism and Existentialism in the nineteenth and twentieth centuries.

Today, especially on our North American continent, we are experiencing a revival in modern form of the classical Greek and Roman idea of education; namely, that education must be "public" (that is, it must be viewed within the context of a political community and ideology). Whether such an ideology is understood in the sense of the views of a John Dewey, Herbert Marcuse, or the Prime Minister of Ontario, William Davis, is basically immaterial and only a difference of degree: they all believe that true education is "public" or to be determined ultimately by the contours of a political community.

Within the context of such an understanding of the fundamental thrust and ultimate aim of education, we have been and are called upon to live and work educationally. How have we as children of the Reformation fared on this score? Let us have a brief and penetrating look at the heritage of Protestant Christianity.

2. Struggle for the survival and self-identity of Christian education: all Christian education is "private"

Having broken away from the Roman Catholic tradition of the Middle Ages and having to ward off the attacks of Humanism and the Renaissance, the Christians of the Reformation were confronted by the challenge of also reforming the area of education in a biblical way. On this score, they did not succeed as well as they did in the institutional churches. Preoccupied as they were with ecclesiastical and confessional issues, and not being able to benefit from a meaningful Christian tradition in education, most Protestants were forced into the situation of having to continue the centuries-old custom of regarding Christian education primarily as the educational ministry of the instituted church. There was but one difference now, however. Whereas before the Reformation there was only one instituted church, there were now many different churches or denominations. The inevitable result of this development was that Christian – still equated with church! – education could no longer be thought of as something that was essentially "public" in nature. Whenever and wherever Roman Catholics and Protestants were in a position to make one church become the state church, the identification of "Christian" and "public" education could be legally enforced. This was historically anti-normative, however. What became and is becoming increasingly more normative in our Western world is that education is public and Christianity is a private affair.

During the sixteenth century a few attempts were made to come up with a more biblical idea of Christian education. These undertakings failed, however, almost as soon as they were started. We can think of the Calvinistic centres of advanced learning in such places as Strassbourg in German, Cracow in Poland, Geneva in Switzerland and Leyden in the Netherlands. These Calvinistic schools were basically not much different from the Lutheran ones in Germany and the Puritan ones in England and New England. In varying degrees, they all remained predominantly educational means of perpetuating the respective ecclesiastical institutions and traditions, and of training the ministers of the Gospel. There was very little, if any, concern with analyzing and effectively counteracting the central thrust of classical education. The traditional curriculum remained intact and beyond the scope of renewal and restoration in Christ. Religion, the Christian religion, Protestant Christian religion is something personal and private. The most one can do – and in fact has been done! – is to add Bible or Theology courses and then to hope and pray that somehow the teaching of the so-called liberal arts may make the Christian youth become better, more intellectual and more cultured members of the church.

It has also continued to be an underlying assumption in the mainstream of Protestant Christianity that life is made up of that which is private and that which is public. This is the erroneous context within which Christians have struggled to discover their own identity and the uniqueness of Christian education. Because most Christians have been incognizant of or unwilling to correct the wrongly assembled outer rim or frame, they have been principally unable to complete the puzzle of Christian education. The contextual framework continued to be the one of private and public, church and state, Christianity and the world, belief and understanding, the Bible and learning, sacred and secular, prayer closet and study room, subjective and objective, sectarianism and tolerance, revelation and nature, faith and reason, heart and mind, piety and science, confession and study, Christ and culture, church and education, and so on.

Many Christian educators sense, intuitively, the error of such an approach. Yet they experience great difficulty extricating themselves from the powerful suction of such a false mentality: after all, doesn't everybody think and act in this unbiblical way!? At the same time, realistic Christians realize that they are gradually losing more and more ground and must be satisfied with less and less freedom to move about in the educational world. Arriving at this critical juncture, a disturbing number of Christians advocate isolation as the best way to ensure orthodoxy. It is this form of systematic retreat by most Christians on which the forces of apostasy are trying to capitalize: secularism becomes more and more public and Christianity more and more private, and vice versa. As far as the cultural power of institutions of higher learning is concerned, the Christian religion has for all practical purposes been sidelined by the forces of unbelief in our post-Christian era.

Perhaps the tide can be stemmed as yet. Christianity can become educationally effective in a more integral and meaningful way than ever before in our Western world. But to do so it will then have to get rid of its religious schizophrenia at the depth level of its existence. This holds true for Roman Catholics, Lutherans, Baptists, Anglicans, Calvinists, Puritans, Congregationalists, Presbyterians, Pietists, Fundamentalists, Anabaptists, Orthodox, Evangelicals and all other Christian groups.

The very history of modern Christianity demands this painful assessment and its religious challenge, I believe, when it comes to the matter of Christian education.

The Search for Integral "Christian Education"

1. Nineteenth-century crisis — Guilluame Groen van Prinsterer and Abraham Kuyper

In line with the great Christian reformers Augustine and Calvin, nineteenth-century Dutch reformers Groen van Prinsterer and Abraham Kuyper moved strategically in the right direction. Both men keenly sensed that the matter of Christian education was part and parcel of a bigger issue, namely, Christian religion, Christian life and Christian culture. Confrontation with a civilization so strangled with a spirit of unbelief (which like an octopus had reached out into every segment of culture and particularly the world of education) demanded, in the estimation of these men, nothing less than the full Gospel of Jesus Christ in all of its ramifications and power. This implied trying to do something positive in a truly Christian way, first of all in the area of education where the leaders of the future have to be trained. It is a question of the Word of God versus the word of man, the Kingdom of God or the *polis* of man.

Guilluame Groen van Prinsterer, sometimes called the founder of the Christian day school movement, had such a radical, all-of-culture-encompassing challenge in mind when he opened the first Christian day school during 1841. Similarly, in Amsterdam, Abraham Kuyper wanted to challenge Humanist scholarship at its roots when he opened the Free University of Amsterdam in 1880. Both men placed the cause of Christian education within the larger context of a Christ-centred reconciliation in the home, in politics, industry, social conditions, journalism and the church. Abraham Kuyper's brilliant insight was to see that Christian education should be free from any external domination of either the church or the state. That is why he spoke on the topic of "Sphere Sovereignty" (*Souvereiniteit in eigen Kring*) during the opening ceremonies of the Free University. Education *itself* must be restructured from within in the light of God's Word. Christian education was not to condone state domination: with this Kuyper stabbed at the very heart of the classical Greek and Roman idea of education! Christian education was not to allow the institutional church to exercise dominion either: with this Kuyper stabbed at the very core of the typical Roman Catholic understanding of Christian (that is, church) education.

2. The Futility of Stop-Gap Measures

Hundreds of Christian schools have been founded. *That* we need Chrisitan education many of us are pretty well convinced. But we cannot stand still. We must advance. It would be a denial of the scriptural vision of earlier reformers if we did not continue where they left off. What Churchill once said during World War II can be repeated here: the end of the beginning may not be the beginning of the end.

We must ask ourselves *what* we mean by Christian education and thus move into a new phase. As we stand at the beginning of this second phase, the fear and trembling of faith grips us – it is no small matter to talk about truly Christian education in the midst of our hyper-secular and anti-Christian era as far as the main forces in our culture are concerned! We are called upon to do battle on two sides at the same time. There is first of all the struggle against the deviousness of apostasy. But there is, secondly, also the battle we must wage against evil forces within the ranks of the Christian community. There is such an appalling confusion among Christians as to what Christian education is all about. There is such a disturbing lack of vision as to the nature and scope of a full-orbed life lived before the face of Yahweh. There is such a frightening division and paralyzing complacency within Christianity at large. There are still so many futile attempts to Christianize education *merely* by organizing spiritual retreats, conducting chapel exercises on campus, devising more Sunday Schools, offering different and additional Bible courses, conducting campus crusades, and so on. These and other attempts, in themselves not necessarily wrong, are to be rejected as mere stop-gap measures if they are intended as substitutes or countermeasures to the cause of true reformation and reformulation of all education at Christ's feet.

Summary and Conclusion

As we look at the past, take our stand in the present, and move into the future with the joy of the Lord, we should remember that:

63

John C. VanderStelt

a. The Greek and Roman idea of education is an expression of a pagan lifestyle.

b. Christian education cannot be obtained, survive and stem the tide of increased secularism in education if Christian education remains essentially nothing more than the education that is performed by, provided for and controlled by institutional churches.

c. Unless Christian colleges and universities continue to work hard and with a profound sense of urgency at reforming and restructuring every aspect of the educational endeavor, there is in the long run very little hope for our elementary and secondary Christian schools, humanly speaking.

d. The initial and ultimate meaning of Christian education is determined not by any church, state or educational institution itself but by the biblical meaning of the Kingdom of God.

e. Only when Christian education comes into its own, beginning to function in the freedom it has under the Word of God, can all the rest of culture, including the institutional churches, truly benefit from the scriptural leaders who have been taught in Christ-centred institutions of higher learning to live as new creatures in the midst of a dark and very complex age.

f. Christian education is but one of the signposts signifying that there is new life. For its survival and development it needs the signposts of the Christian home, Christian church, Christian politics, Christian fine arts, Christian industry and business, and so on. If this is a dream then it is a dream of faith — of a faith that leads to the action demonstrating the fact that God in Christ is reconciling the world unto Himself. Anything else is also a dream — a dream of death filled with the horror of God-forsakenness. It is a dream which haunts our modern universities — a desperate, groping search for meaning which cannot be found through solely human efforts.

But the Saviour said, "My PEACE I leave with you!"

3

*THE CURRICULUM AS GUIDELINE
IN CHRIST-CENTERED
LIVING AND LEARNING*

Towards a Radical Break with the Public School Curriculum

by Harro Van Brummelen

Recent Trends in the Curriculum of the Public School

North American society has always expected a great deal of education and has expressed great faith in it as "the life-giving principle of national power," to use Walter Lippmann's phrase. Most North Americans believe that education must promote the American Way of Life – as was shown by the hue and cry that went up about the quality of education in 1957 after Russia launched its first Sputnik. American prestige was at stake. Scholars, educators and teachers all became involved in what was hailed as a revolution in education. This revolution would cause education once again to become the chief instrument for enlightenment and progress.

However, today society realizes that this revolution has failed. What are the reasons for this failure? First of all, curriculum development has not been guided by any comprehensive concept of the process of education. Pieces of the curriculum were shifted and replaced without a reappraisal of the whole pattern. Rather than starting with the question *why* we should teach certain topics, the foremost question became *how* we could teach the maximum number of concepts and skills in the minimum period of time. Instead of giving positive direction in teaching students how to grapple with the problems that deal with the warp and woof of today's culture, today's curriculum is abstract and removed from the child's everyday experience. Rather than preparing his for *life,* the curriculum prepares him for even more specialized courses in university or at technical institutes.

As a result, the faith that education and national progress would continue to lead hand-in-hand to a better world has eroded. Since the new curricula have not led to a new utopia, schools are coming under increasing critical scrutiny. It has become a cliche to say that schools face a crisis. There is anxiety that modern education is adrift without rudder, chart, or compass.

Leaders in education have become aware of this and articles in professional journals have recently become more and more concerned with the basic goals and objectives of the school. Unfortunately, nearly all proposals for change fall once again into the trap of John Dewey's pragmatism. Pragmatism preaches that the meaning of things is to be found in their usefulness. If a process works, then it becomes the morally right thing to do. The child is looked upon as a potential creator of values in a given environment, and there is a tremendous faith in the individual and in democracy, an invincible belief in human progress and the perfectibility of man. The child must live in, for, and by society – in order to work together with others along common lines in a common spirit and with reference to a common aim. But this common aim is experimental, always tested in action. The norm becomes, "Let's keep experimenting o see what will work; human nature is basically good and education facilitates growth to a more perfect human society, one in which human wants will be fully satisfied."

But the question becomes, "What values do we have in common in our democratic society?" The public school curriculum has answered that one of the most important common threads in the fabric of our society is the *scientific method;* it holds that you can reach conclusions from unbiased observations of the phenomena around you. This method is assumed to be *the* way to the truth in all areas of life – science, psychology, sociology, economics, ethics. But the humanist forgets that the method is not common to all men or even all scientists, for different people interpret it differently; nor is it the only method, nor, in fact, even the most important method used in the sciences. Moreover, it cannot lead us to the truth, since its final authority is not God's revelation, but man's observation. Yet the scientific method has become a pseudo-god in the curriculum, giving a wrong and one-sided view of the structure of creation; it is assumed to determine all things in life.

At the same time, the humanist curriculum sways back and forth between going discipline-centred on the one hand *or* child-centred on the other hand. In the first case, human reason becomes a false idol which replaces the Word of God as the Truth. In the child-centred school, human personality becomes the idol: whatever interests the child becomes a value worthy of being pursued, and in this way the child supposedly searches for the "truth," and his "god" often becomes the scientific method and technology. In both cases the school is man-centred rather than Christ-centred.

Public education has a faith commitment to which a Christian cannot adhere. There is no room in the public school for the Christian as an *integral* Christian. A Christian in the public school cannot be wholly faithful to Christ's command of Matthew 29: "Go to peoples everywhere and make them by disciples. . .teach them to obey everything I have commanded you." As Christians we will necessarily be at loggerheads with the basic aims of the public school and the way these aims are embodied in its curriculum. We can develop a Christian mind, we can teach

Harro Van Brummelen

students to think Christianly about the issues that face us, *only* if we first of all develop an overall view of Christian education and structure our curriculum accordingly.

What, then, are the main steps in forging a Christian curriculum? There are at least four steps before we are able to sit down and write specific units for various courses:

First, we must determine the basis and foundation of the curriculum and its ultimate goals.

Second, we must study the demands and requirements of our present-day culture and the Christian's task within that culture, and analyze the implications for the curriculum.

Third, we must examine the nature of knowledge; the specific characteristics and unique contributions of the various disciplines, how the disciplines are interrelated, and the nature of analytic thought.

Fourth, we must examine the nature of the child; how he develops, how he learns, and how we can organize the school and the classroom in order that it will help rather than hinder us in meeting the objectives of the curriculum.

If our curriculum is to be an integrally Christian one, we can determine more specific aims for various parts of the curriculum and write units for the classroom only *after* these four steps have been considered. I want to examine each of these steps in some detail, and then discuss tentative models for the elementary and high school curriculum.

The Basis of the Curriculum and Its Ultimate Goals

The Christian curriculum must help the student to love the Lord our God with all his heart and soul and strength. Through the curriculum he must learn to discern the Truth which is Christ. As Jesus said, "Let the children come unto me; do not try to stop them; for the Kingdom of Heaven belongs to such as these." We cannot determine the student's heart commitment, but we *can* structure the curriculum so that the faith that *is* present is fostered, and show what faith is and how it encompasses and directs our lives.

A curriculum that is obedient to God's revelation in the Scriptures starts with the recognition that, as John says, the Word structures all creation. "All that came to be was alive with his life, and that life was the light of men. The light shines on in the dark, and the darkness never mastered it. . .grace and truth came through Jesus Christ." We must show the students that everywhere around them God reveals Himself. As Paul says in Romans 1, ". . .For all that may be known of God by men lies plain before their eyes; indeed God Himself has disclosed it to them. His invisible attributes, that is to say his everlasting power and deity, have been visible, ever since the world began, to the eye of reason, in the things He has made." Or, as the psalmist exclaims, "How clearly the sky reveals God's glory! How plainly it shows what He has done!" The curriculum must direct our thoughts to the works of God in creation. It must show that God is a faithful God who through His grace in Jesus Christ maintains and upholds the law structures that we discover.

Also, the curriculum must show that God through His Spirit lays claim on our *whole* life; the Word calls each one of us to obedience and complete allegiance. Paul points out in I Corinthians that this world's wisdom is foolishness, and that it is impossible for men to know him by means of their own wisdom. God has made Christ to be our wisdom through the power of the Spirit; by Him we are put right with God, we become God's own people, and are set free so that we may start to carry out life's calling.

The curriculum is the plan for learning that translates what we as Christians know about man and his calling into a specific program of courses in the school. The curriculum aims at preparing the student for a life of faith in the community so that the Christian school becomes a culture-forming force in our society. Our cultural mandate is clear — we must develop and unfold our world, open up God's creation. The ultimate goal of Christian education is to equip the student for living a Christian life in today's culture so that by God's grace he will be ready to respond to God's calling.

Characteristics of Today's Society: Implications for the Curriculum

Man feels powerful and autonomous in today's secular society. Despite rumblings from prophets of doom, the belief in human perfectibility and an optimism about improving people as well as the human condition remains part and parcel of the democratic creed. The dominant role of science and technology has led to material wealth but spiritual poverty. Our culture fills up its great amount of leisure time with pursuits that are effortless and comfortable, and there is no time for family life, communal discussions, thoughtful reflection, communication with God; in other words, there is no time for the important things in life. Events and actions follow each other rapidly, causing variety in our lives but also anxiety and uneasiness.

The paradox of the humanist is that he has constructed a complex social machine to administer the technical machine he has built, but his whole "creation" stands over and above him and manipulates him. As a result, man, and especially youth, has become alienated from the society he has built. A reaction against our sterile culture has set in — breakdown of authority, skepticism, protest, drugs, astrology, sexual deviations, various liberation movements, and reactions against scientism and individualism.

At the same time, the Gospel has become irrelevant for modern culture. Our society has lost its Christian signature. The church has little influence except on people's personal lives. Even many evangelical Christians consider it strangely out-of-place if a politician or a newspaper writer or a TV commentator or a milkman or a housewife would consider their tasks within an integral Christian framework.

Such is the concrete spiritual and practical situation for which we have to prepare our students for their life's calling. In a dynamic culture, the curriculum must show that our anchor is the knowledge that all creation has a religious character pointing beyond this creation to God. The curriculum's task is to take the student and make his profession of Christianity a significant one – one which gives him the means to express a responsible human citizenship in the Kingdom of God. The curriculum must lead the student through the various "rooms" in God's creation so that he can take upon himself the task that God has given him at creation: to subdue the earth and have dominion over it in love and obedience to God.

Because Christ redeemed the world, mankind can unfold the plan of God in His creation. However, sin and its consequences affect all human activity. Sin and redemption are intertwined – also in the work of the Christian community and in our own hearts. But because modern culture has lost sight completely of the Kingdom of God, the curriculum must show the student that the Christian cannot become an integral part of modern culture; we must be *in* the world but not *of* the world; our task is to build a Christian culture.

To do this *and* be relevant in our present age, the curriculum must lead the student to a deeper understanding of our modern society. He must be made aware of the historical roots of our civilization as well as of the present value systems, the aims and ideals, the ultimate loyalties and allegiances of Western culture. This means that the curriculum must deal with the ideas of the Greeks, with philosophers such as Sartre and Marcuse, with the themes of today's rock music, with modern novels, with modern art, with modern science and technology. The student must learn to differentiate between what is acceptable and what is unacceptable in our society, what must be developed, what must be reformed.

Also, the curriculum must show the student that today's society is a constantly changing one, where new problems will face him regularly. He will live in a civilization in which tension and conflict are increasing as it turns further away from God. He must understand God's abiding biblical norms so that he can apply and adapt them to the new situations he will face continually.

The curriculum must teach students that we have to witness both individually and communally to the powers that rule our universe, and that where necessary we must work at developing Christian alternatives. The curriculum must foster the idea of a Christian community, for we as Christians must not stand alone in the world; we are part of the body of believers. The child has his own unique gifts which must be developed in order to contribute to that body. Students should be taught to listen to *each other,* learn to know and understand each other, work together in trust, open up to each other, learn to help each other. If this is introduced systematically, it may help to overcome selfish individualism and consolidate Christians into a culturally formative, witnessing community. We are members of one body who need to strengthen each other in our common task.

The Nature of Knowledge and Theoretical Thought: Implications for the Curriculum

Knowledge cannot be neutral. Behind all knowledge lies a principial vision on the basis of which the known facts and realities are explained. All learning takes place within a certain framework. As Christians, we accept the Bible's revelation that God is the creator of heaven and earth and that we can gather knowledge about creation because God has made His creation a structured unity which He, for Christ's sake, despite the fall of man, maintains and upholds. The curriculum must show the student that man has received freedom to fulfil his calling in the service of God, his neighbour, creation, and himself within the law structures that He has laid down in creation. These laws are manifold and pervasive; they are the basis for the way we multiply numbers, for the movement of the planets, for the growth of a plant, for the way our economy operates, for the interaction between a boy and a girl in love, for the way we compose and appreciate music. To gain true insight, we must submit ourselves to God's revelation of His structural laws in creation.

One major weakness of the present curriculum is that there is an almost total lack of insight into the interrelationship of the various disciplines. Our curriculum must provide the student with a sense of unity and purpose, a sense of their many-sided calling, a sense of their responsibility to God, to the Christian community, to the world. It is not the task of the school to create specialists. Some of our students will undoubtedly become specialists in their later life — but we must teach them that they may not neglect relating specific knowledge to the overall situation. The curriculum must teach them to ask, "How does my specialty affect other areas of knowledge and the whole of life? How can I be responsible in using my speciality in contributing to the enrichment of human culture? How does my discipline contribute to a meaningful outlook on the future of society?"

The present curriculum is concerned mainly with techniques and the teaching of facts for the sake of cataloging knowledge — with the possible exception of the social studies and English programs. The danger of such specialization can be seen from an example. There is a mathematical technique called linear programming which is used by large industrial concerns to determine the most efficient method of operation – leading to maximum profit. The approach used by my grade eleven text is this: here is a technique used in industry; learn it and apply it to the following seven problems. Unlike most exercises, the problems did present situations that were not completely abstract and at least dealt with situations that the students could visualize occurring in everday life. But, on the other hand, the implication of the section was that the mathematician is concerned *only* with the mathematical technique, and not at all with the other aspects of the situation. That a company should maximize its profit by hook or crook was a tacit assumption. The mathematician does not concern himself with the physical and biological side of the situation. It is not mentioned that maximizing profit might mean that our resources are depleted unnecessarily or that it might upset the ecology. Nor does he concern himself with the psychological or social aspects. Might he create unnecessary tensions between workers by putting this into affect? Or the juridical aspect – might he break the spirit if not the letter of certain of the government's laws? Or the ethical aspect – is it right to expect workers to have to work overtime or to be laid off at will? By maximizing profit is the worker being reduced to a robot who cannot fulfill his calling before the face of the Lord?

Present mathematics courses imply that these are questions that must stay far from the mathematician's mind. He is a technician, not a philosopher. The Christian curriculum, when teaching such a technique, must look at all these aspects so that the student learns to think analytically about his task as prophet, priest, and king within the community, and how he can perform this task within the total industrial situation.

At the same time, even though we can list many properties of any given situations that the student can learn to analyze and discover, and of which he can realize some implications, we must recognize that our knowledge of creation is much fuller than the analytic properties we can perceive and analyze. Knowledge cannot be identified with or reduced to analytic inquiry.

Let me give another example. We can analyze the concept of "fire" in many different ways. The physicist can explain why a flame has a certain color. The chemist can describe it using a chemical equation. For a northern trapper, fire means survival. The great fire of Chicago is historically important. Fire has an aesthetic dimension; we appreciate the beauty of flames dancing in the night. It has a social function in that it creates a certain atmosphere around a fireplace or campfire. Fire is an economic necessity in our modern society, but also causes economic dislocation. Fire has a religious significance – recall the burning bush, or the flames signifying the pouring out of Christ's Spirit. I could go on and probably write a whole book about the various aspects. But when I'm done, I still haven't gotten at the essence of fire; it's a far more complex and deeper phenomenon than we can analyze.

God's creation-structure exhibits a fullness and diversity that is impossible to grasp or understand completely with our analytical thought. The student must learn to realize that while analytical thinking allows him to gain insight into many situations, his experiential knowledge of creation – including such concepts as faith, love, and justice – is deeper than the part that can be explained using his analytical reasoning. And even with experiential knowledge, we see through a glass darkly.

However, despite the limitations of analytical thinking, the school's task is to develop the sutdent's analytical functioning so that both the unity and the diversity of God's universe become clear to him. Knowledge is never an end in itself. The student must learn to discern the Truth that is Christ and at the same time evaluate and judge the religious alliances of mankind so that he will be able to grasp the full significance of what it means to lead a full-orbed life for Christ.

The Nature of the Child and of Education

The question "What is man?" is the unavoidable preamble to the Christian view of education. Man is and remains the crown of creation, an image bearer of the Lord, called to respond to God's Word. But even though a child is a responsible human creature, he does not develop automatically, but must be guided and led by a teacher using sound pedagogical, formative methods. The teacher must give direction to the development of the student, unfolding him toward a certain goal according to biblical norms. Our forming must lead to self-responsibility in taking up life's calling.

At the same time, the child remains a free, responsible human subject whose opinions and reactions must be respected even if sometimes not approved. A teacher must be concerned about the child's development and allow him the emotional freedom to respond to the teacher's guidance in his own unique way; to state his own views, to experiment, to investigate, to search and probe for answers. We must ensure that the curriculum is structured to allow for this, and organize the school and the classroom accordingly. This is such an important aspect of Christian education that the next chapter will deal with it, and therefore I will not elaborate at this time.

Towards a Radical Break with the Public School Curriculum

The Structure of the Curriculum

Since the ultimate goal of Christian education is to equip the student to respond positively to God's calling in all areas of life, the curriculum must prepare our students for the tasks and responsibilities that he now faces and that lie ahead. He must learn to function in his own unique, responsible way in such things as showing Christian troth in marriage and the family; exercising his responsibility as a voter and citizen as well as in the world of work; using his God-given economic resources in a responsible way both personally and in business; helping to form a Christian mind with respect to concepts such as justice, freedom, sexuality, and the welfare state; appreciating the necessity of developing Christian approaches to art, music, the mass media, the use of leisure time; having a Christian consciousness with respect to the poor, the sick, the aged, the emotionally ill, and minority groups. For all this the student must have an understanding of the biblical norms for life as well as of the underlying religious motives of our culture.

The big question is, "How can the curriculum accomplish this?" I will show tentative models first for the elementary and then for the high school curriculum.

The Elementary School Curriculum

The elementary school should have an integrated curriculum with social studies, science, reading materials, mathematics, Bible history, and art, all interrelated. A start on such a curriculum was made in the summer of 1971-72 in Toronto and the first experimental units of an integrated curriculum for the lower grades have been mimeographed, tested and revised. Starting with God's plan for creation, man's disobedience and his new start in Christ, the next units deal with the earth, man's home —

THE ELEMENTARY SCHOOL CURRICULUM: A MODEL FOR DISCUSSION

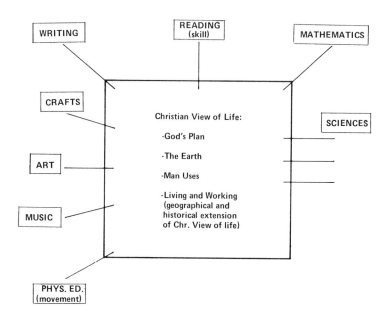

From a working paper in the
OACS/AACS Summer Workshop
Program, 1971.

the realm of physical things, plants, and animals. The emphasis throughout is on man hearing God's voice and answering it in his way of life; man is a religious creature who takes care (or neglects to take care) of the physical, plant, and animal realms, and man must serve God by using, developing, and preserving His creation. This is integrated with mathematics (graphs, sizes, measurement); with reading (poems and articles about sounds, colours, plants, animals); with biblical themes (the creation story, parables, Psalm 104); with writing assignments (write a story about a dandelion seed, about a day in the life of a plant); with art, music, and crafts. Also, it is shown how the various realms of reality are interrelated. For example, the sun provides energy for grass to grow; the cow eats the grass and provides milk for man so that he can be healthy to perform his tasks.

This is followed by units that consider in greater depth how man uses, develops, and cares for creation, and how man lives and works together in the family, state, church, and business. By grade four, it could be shown how man has responded to his mandate in specific instances; for example, the Eskimos, Indians, explorers, and settlers. By grades six and seven this would be expanded to indicate some of the cultural ideals of Western civilization. All of this will be unified around the theme that God has given one task to all people; that the one task has many parts; that man has spoiled the creation; but that God has given man a new start in Christ.

Ideally — and this is still some time away in most schools — the teacher would arrange the classroom environment in such a way that the student would do many tasks on his own or work in small groups. In such an environment where a child investigates, analyzes, discovers, experiences, reads, discusses, relates, and cooperates with others, it is of the utmost importance that the learning situations are well structured and interrelate so that the

Towards a Radical Break with the Public School Curriculum

student gains an awareness of reality as God's world in which man has a special task. Already in the earliest grades the child must be led to see that believers in Christ have individual and communal callings in our culture, but that at the same time sin is a conquered but no less real force both within and without the Christian community.

The High School Curriculum

The high school curriculum must also become far more unified in purpose and direction. The tentative model shows a curriculum that differs greatly from the present high school curriculum which usually is a collection of individual, unrelated courses. This model would serve for grades eight or nine to twelve. It tries to stress the interdependence of all our disciplines, for it is impossible to go very deeply in any one discipline without striking at the roots of another.

It is for this reason that at the centre you see a basic "core" course, which has at its base biblical studies which are aimed at exploring and determining the concrete biblical norms that govern our lives. In the same course, directly connected with this biblical basis, there are a variety of units discussing the church; family and marriage; justice and the political state; the place of music and art in culture; labour, business, and consumer economics; social issues such as poverty, racial and ethnic relations, cities and city life; the means of communication in our society (magazines, mass media, advertising); structuring our environment both as a society and as individuals (hunger, pollution, transportation, housing, health); and the impact of technology that has mechanized and standardized life. All these topics must tie in directly with the study of Bible — otherwise the student does not integrate biblical principles in his everyday life or applies them only in a moralistic way. As a student progresses through the grades,

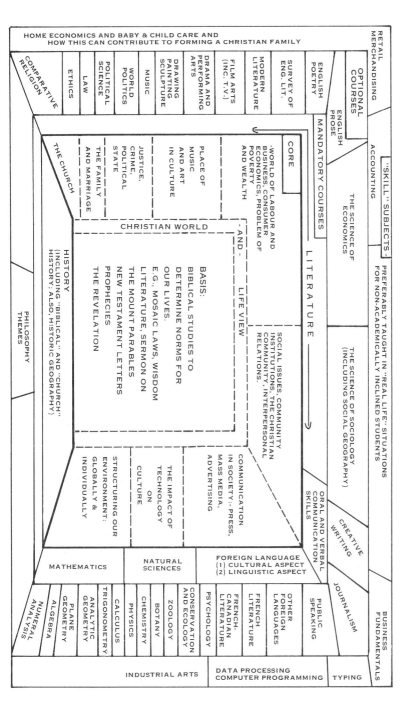

THE HIGH SCHOOL CURRICULUM: A TENTATIVE MODEL FOR DISCUSSION

he will study such topics as the Mosaic laws, the wisdom literature and the prophets, the sermon on the mount and the parables, the New Testament letters, and the book of Revelation — all within the context of the covenant relationship and the coming of the Kingdom. From this, awareness of God's plan for creation and man's cultural mandate will increase, and gradually the core topics can be studied in more depth, particularly in grade twelve.

This core course together with the history course forms the central focus of the curriculum, and all other courses — mandatory and optional — must relate directly to this inner core. This is the course that deserves the most immediate attention of the whole Christian community, and it is one in which all the teachers of a school should participate. It should be planned and developed and taught by the staff as a team, with everyone contributing in one area or another.

The *history course* is included in the inner core "square," but is a separate course. History in the Christian school must incorporate as an integral part redemptive, biblical history as well as Church history. If these are taught separately, it suggests to the student that biblical and Church history events are disjoined from the rest of history, that we as Christians stand outside of "regular" history. We must stress that *all* of history shows the Spirit of God at work and man unfolding God's creation. The cultural development of Old Testament Israel shows the social unfolding of God's chosen people, pointing forward to Christ, who is the focus of history. We must show in the regular history course how Christians have influenced (or failed to influence) the development of Western thought, and what the relationship of the Church has been to culture.

History must be included in the curriculum as a core course because students cannot understand the forces at work in today's society without coming to grips with the historic roots of our culture. Human ideals and values have been positive or negative responses to our creation mandate, and the student must learn to discern the development of Humanism from the Greeks to the Renaissance to the present day. And he cannot understand today's humanistic concepts of the democratic way of life, of individualism, of the preeminence of pragmatism in politics and business, unless he understands the mixture of Humanism and Christianity, the mixture of sin and redemption, the mixture of ignoring God or listening to Him, that have been at work in Western civilization. All this must be seen in the light of the return of Christ and the establishment of His Kingdom.

Thus the core of history focuses on the spiritual struggles of the past as they affect the present. However, the historical side of each discipline should also be stressed in each of the mandatory and optional courses. A course like world politics can be meaningful only if the historical aspect is given a central place. In mathematics and science, a historical approach gives the student a feeling of how man developed and unfolded God's creation, and that this process is still continuing and that he has a calling to help in this task. An understanding of the history of each discipline is an essential key to enable the student to discern and evaluate the religious alliances that shaped our culture.

Each student is required to take a number of *mandatory courses.* These courses relate directly to the core, and rather than *stressing* technical skills (although some basic ones would be taught), the main goal of these courses would be to come to an understanding of some of the basic structures of the discipline, of the place of the discipline within the structure of creation, how it developed through history, and how it is used and misused in today's society.

Let me give another example from my own subject

area. Mathematics is the science which investigates and describes the numerical and spatial aspects of the universe around us. Our students must learn to see that we use mathematics as a functional tool to develop and preserve the creation, and thus to build up God's Kingdom. Mathematics may never be pursued as an end in itself. It must contribute to a better management of creation with God's Word as our guide, giving us a sense of purpose and direction. Mathematics must be shown as a developing science which throughout history has influenced and is influenced by cultural forces.

We abstract the mathematical properties of a certain situation in the created reality we observe, think analytically about these properties, deepen our understanding of them, but in the end we must apply the results by considering the whole situation and all the aspects it involves. Thus mathematics helps us to solve everyday problems and to explain the quantitative aspects of situations we face. Almost all major fields of human endeavour and innumerable situations in everyday life are likely to lead to significant applications of mathematics. Such applications should be an integral part of the mathematics program – yet those of you who are familiar with present high school mathematics courses know that students are never shown *why* they should learn factoring or prove identities nor how these topics enable us to understand our creation and fulfill our cultural mandate as a community.

To use a musical analogy, what we do in mathematics today is like teaching students how to play the C major musical scale and then telling him to practice this for three years. At the end, he will know how to play the C major scale extremely fast and very accurately, but he will not appreciate music nor be a musician. Yet this is what we are doing in mathematics and in other subject areas as well – we create specialized technicians, dodging the foundational questions, not showing the relevance of what we are doing.

Through his study of mathematics, the student should gain respect for the laws which hold for God's creation order. It is no accident that four ten-cent chocolate bars cost 40c. There is a certain "universal validity" to these laws; they are dependable and can be trusted deeply. Even though we make mistakes and errors in our theorizing, reality is harmoniously and integrally "consistent." Keeping this in mind, the student should become aware of the power as well as the limitations of mathematics. Try as he may, good intentions (or bad ones) will not change the law structure of creation. The student should be led to trust the dependability of God upholding these law structures.

The mandatory mathematics couse would emphasize the development and place of mathematics in Western culture, its relationship to the physical and biological and economic and aesthetic aspects of reality. The optional course would still have the same objectives, but develop topics in much greater depth for students having a special interest in mathematics.

The second mandatory course would be science. Again, the aim of this course would be to lead the student to realize that the world is a cosmos rather than a chaos, and that the order we discover is a created structural order rooted in Christ. The student must come to realize that science — including the scientific method — has a rightful place but that its place is limited and may not be deified. They must learn to see that "facts" have meaning only if they are placed in a perspective or framework and that values are embedded in reality itself. Foundational questions may not be dodged and should be discussed with different degrees of thoroughness at different age levels. And this starts already in grade one when, for instance, a child might ask about life and death because his pet hamster died.

Harro Van Brummelen

A foreign language — in English Canada, it should be French — should be mandatory for several years, with a two-fold emphasis. The linguistic structure will show the student how there are laws governing the way people communicate. Secondly, the cultural aspect will demonstrate how language draws people together into a community and how language and culture interrelate and develop together; language is *more* than a tool for communication. In Canada this task is especially important because almost daily we are confronted with the question of French/English relations. Students must learn to understand the Quebec culture through their study of French.

Literature should be closely connected with the core course, because literature reveals how the laws of creation operate in concrete life situations. The scope of literature is wide; in studying literature you are always dealing with life. Literature in the curriculum must not only be chosen because of its technical excellence and creativity, but also because of its value in leading the student to a deeper understanding of our culture and society, so that his Christian sensitivity and insight into the topics listed in the core are increased. In our present day and age, non-Christian authors often have more to tell us about our culture than Christian ones.

Somewhere in the curriculum, students must be taught the mechanics of communicating verbally and orally. Such a course can be short, for the student should develop his communication skills in his other courses. This would involve especially literature and the core course, but there is a place for essays and oral reports in mathematics and science, too.

In short, the mandatory courses would develop some basic skills that the students need to live in today's society; show them the effect of the subject on culture and vice versa; enable them to see the unity of reality within the

Towards a Radical Break with the Public School Curriculum

many diverse but related aspects; and show them how they must use reality to unfold and enrich our lives in relation to man's cultural mandate.

I have shown some possible optional courses in the next rectangle. This list is not meant to be exhaustive. Options could be short, two-month studies of a particular topic or a longer in-depth investigation, giving students flexibility in their program. As for the mandatory courses, the objectives of options should tie in with those of the core course, and the stress would be analytical rather than informational. Several such courses – such as themes of philosophy and ethics – could not be taught until grade twelve except for very mature students. Non-academically inclined students would study the core and mandatory courses, but would learn skills like the ones shown in the outer rectangle for a large part of the day, especially in higher grades. Rather than the school teaching these skills, it would be preferable if such skills were taught "on the job," that is, in business establishments and homes. Only the basic principles and the perspective in which those skills must be viewed would be taught in the school.

Conclusion

It is clear by now that educators face a mammoth task and need the help and prayer of the whole Christian community. We need the insights of philosophers, psychologists, and various subject specialists. I am happy that there are plans for starting a curriculum centre in Toronto, and I hope that this will become an international centre for the development and implementation of an integral Christian curriculum, working in close liaison with the National Union of Christian Schools and other associations of Christian schools.

We must break radically with the humanistic curriculum of the public school. All true teaching aims to

Harro Van Brummelen

teach mankind how to take sides — and the public school's side is the side of secular Humanism. Let us in humility try to structure our curriculum so that it shows our students that Jesus Christ is the Way, the Truth, and the Life and that it teaches them to serve Him in their lives.

Building a Curriculum with the Kingdom Vision

by John Van Dyk

In the early 1970's curriculum studies occupied a major place in the educational enterprise of North America. The rest of this decade, no doubt, will see an even greater stress on curriculum analysis and revision. Numerous graduate schools conduct programs in curriculum development. Publishers produce volume after volume on the history, nature, and future of the curriculum. Large numbers of school systems engage the services of curriculum consultants. Self-styled experts on curriculum are a dime a dozen.

This state of affairs forces the question upon us of where we — as Christians concerned about Christian education — stand on the matter of curriculum. Is there a need for a clear-cut direction towards a truly Christian curriculum, or is it sufficient that our Christian elementary schools, high schools, and colleges be mere adaptations of examples and models to be found in the secular institutions? In other words, is the matter of a Christian curriculum worth discussing?

Curriculum is the Educational Program

In order to be sure that we understand each other, let me first of all briefly state what I mean by the term *curriculum.* Very simply, curriculum refers to the educational program in a school, the course of studies through which the student must travel in order to graduate. Curriculum, therefore, involves the selection and arrangement of subject matter which is to be taught in such a way that certain specific educational goals are attained. In this essay I will address myself to the areas of subject matter and educational goals. I leave out, then, the whole matter of instructional technique and child development, questions which – although integral to a full-orbed theory of curriculum – will be taken up again in the next chapter.

Eighty Years of Curriculum in North America

Eighty years ago in North America there was no systematic thinking on curriculum matters. Schools in the nineteenth century were staffed by individual teachers teaching individual subject matter from individual textbooks. There was little – if any – coherence and consistency. Teachers required pupils to memorize the content of the textbook. When the pupils became teachers, they in turn required the same memorization from *their* pupils. It was generally believed at that time that such rote learning constituted the most effective method of training the child's mind.

Meanwhile, in that same nineteenth century, Europe, especially Germany, represented the height of scholarship. American college students, eager to exercise their brilliant minds, flocked to Germany to drink deeply from the wells of learning. With their return to America, a variety of German educational theories began to be imported into the new world. So it was that in the 1890's and early 1900's curriculum studies in North America were stirred into existence.

Especially in the years after World War I, more and

more emphasis came to be placed on curriculum studies. It became clear that to teach a variety of subject matter for no reason at all was not in the best interest of meaningful education. Educational theorists began to understand that the curriculum must be carefully designed if the schools were to produce loyal and enthusiastic citizens in the North American democracy. As a result of this awareness, widespread revision of school curricula took place in the twenties and thirties.

It is essential to observe that the curriculum was not just a purely technical matter. On the contrary, school curriculums were designed to implement a way of life! At the same time the converse was true; the American Way of Life demanded a certain kind of curriculum. Keep in mind, then, that curriculum and a way of life go together.

The economic pressures and the resulting social upheavals of the early thirties further stimulated extensive educational research designed to construct new curricula which would be able to cope with the situation. The all-important questions were, "How can our American democracy survive? How can we ensure that our society will not collapse altogether?" The result was a strong stress on social studies, to make sure that school graduates would emerge as mature and well-adjusted citizens.

Throughout the years of the Second World War and the decade following, the emphasis reamined on building the American Way of Life. Democracy was in the air. The Nazis had demonstrated to what atrocious lengths a bigoted gang of men could go. After the War communism provided the example of slavery and oppression. America must be different! America must show the world that the ideal of the Democratic Way of Life is really workable!

In 1957 the launching of the Russian sputnik touched curriculum studies to the core. A clamor was heard throughout the land, "Why has there been so little stress on the study of mathematics and natural science?"

John Van Dyk

Everywhere throughout the North American educational world there was an instant response by switching the emphasis in the curriculum away from the humanities and social studies to mathematics, natural sciences, and foreign languages; math and science to enable America to compete with Russia in the space race; foreign languages to equip America to carry on dialogue with the international world in the Cold War.

As the sixties rolled along, new shifts in curriculum emphasis appeared as new stresses began to bear down on North America. Soon it became evident that the primary challenge for the U.S.A. lay not in creating the ultimate weapon nor in the conquest of the moon, but in coping with the internal problems of racial strife, poverty, and a rebellious youth. Suddenly it became glaringly clear that the American Way of Life was in trouble again. The great American dream was under attack, not by some foreign power, but by internal forces. Once again the effect on the curriculum was felt immediately. Natural sciences, for example, came to be associated with military weapons and industrial superpower. As the unpopular Vietnam War lingered on, increasing numbers of young people, and older ones as well, bitterly criticized the stress on natural sciences in the school curriculum. At the same time the heyday of foreign languages ground to a halt. Foreign languages came to be the symbol of U.S. interference abroad, a symbol of American preoccupation with foreign affairs at the expense of internal peace and justice. Consequently science and math, as well as foreign languages began to lose their status as centre of the curriculum. On the college and university level such fields as sociology, anthropology, and psychology became enormously popular as people sought to find solutions to the problems of our society through research in these areas. Other fields attracted students as well. The study of religion, for example, drew all kinds of people questing for an inner peace which appeared to have receded more and more into distant places.

In the last few years the curriculum has come under greater attack than ever before. It is becoming clearer to ever-increasing numbers of people that somehow our well-constructed curricula miss the boat somewhere. Students openly militate against the irrelevance and meaninglessness of much learning that they must do, especially at the high school, college, and university levels. Educators of all kinds, meanwhile, are at each other's throats. The beautifully constructed curricula designed in the thirties, forties, and fifties have not brought about the American dream of a great united community. Instead, our land has gone from crisis to crisis; meanwhile, hatred, racism, immorality, greed, vice, poverty, violence – these continue unabated.

There are Christian schools in our land. Thank the Lord for the work and sacrifice of our fathers and forefathers as they struggled to get the Christian school movement off the ground in North America. We can never be too thankful for what those pioneers of Christian education have been able to accomplish, by the grace of God. Our task is now to carry on that great work, especially now in the seventies, a time in which North America needs the Christian school so desperately. Our task, more than ever, in our turbulent civilization, is to bring the healing power of our Lord to bear on our land in the area of education. And that inevitably involves the curriculum. Let me ask again; where do we, as Christians concerned about Christian education – more than that, as Christians struggling for the coming of God's Kingdom – where do we stand on the matter of the curriculum? Is it going to be enough in the seventies that our Christian schools merely adopt the everchanging curricular patterns from the secular world and put some Christian wrappings around them? Indeed, is Jesus Christ the Lord and Master of the curriculum as well?

John Van Dyk

The Effects of Dualism on Curriculum

The chapter on the history of education explained how too much of Christian education has been dualistic in nature. How has this dualism affected the Christian school curriculum?

Too often, it seems to me, the curriculum of the Christian school has simply been taken over from non-Christian schools, then baptized, so to speak, by means of additional Bible courses and chapel exercises. After all, math is math and French is French, just the same everywhere, whether taught in the Christian or the Jewish or the public school. The result of this approach has been that a variety of secular theories have crept right into the Christian school via the subject matter, and have been palmed off as Christian learning. Thus often, in stealthy fashion, secularism has been propagated – usually unconsciously and inwittingly – by the Christian schools. This is a harsh judgment, I know. Nevertheless it is exceedingly crucial that we recognize this state of affairs. I am convinced that one reason why increasing numbers of Christian school graduates do not send their own children to the Christian school is that they have intuitively recognized – through their own experience as students in our schools – that the curriculum in many instances is not sufficiently different from that of the secular public school to warrant the great financial sacrifice involved.

Our Approach to a Christian Curriculum

How shall we develop a really integral Christian curriculum for our Christian schools and colleges? Can we do this simply by juggling and rejuggling the various areas of subject matter and introducing advanced teaching techniques? Will a Christian school curriculum simply be a matter of deciding what subject to teach at which level?

98

Building a Curriculum with the Kingdom Vision

Here the demon of pragmatism lurks around the corner. Pragmatism has been a dominant philosophy in American education. Pragmatism seeks to implement only that which is workable and that which is efficient, without coming to grips with the really basic principial questions. Pragmatists are therefore always adrift.

I believe that all curriculum revision in the Christian school will tend to be quite meaningless unless we have first of all come to grips with two fundamental questions. Unless we arrive at some clarity on these two basic issues, much of our curriculum work will only be so much patchwork.

Fundamental Issue Number One: Vision

The first question is; What will be the guiding vision that steers the curriculum? Or, to put it a little differently, what world-and-life view determines the goals of our curriculum? What ideal do we want our curriculum to advance?

Let us examine, by way of example, the ideal and the vision that directs the typical North American secular school — whether on the elementary, secondary, or college level. Men, according to this humanistic vision, are rational products of a long evolutionary process. They are free, autonomous individuals whose challenge it is to gain ever more control of nature. And what is nature? No more than a world of matter and atoms functioning according to inherent natural laws. Men, meanwhile, direct their own destiny. They create their own social order according to their own rational insight. *They* decide what government, marriage, and economic activity shall be. As biological organisms, endowed with reason and certain basic needs, men decide what is to be considered good and what is to be considered bad. Such decisions, of course, are to be made democratically.

John Van Dyk

Now observe how this humanistic vision affects the curriculum. (1) First there are the natural sciences, designed to give the pupil some understanding of that factual world of matter run by natural law, from which he has developed, and over which he must gain technological control. (2) Then there are the social and behavioral sciences, designed to explain how men as rational beings order their society and are to order it in accordance with the ideal of a harmonious American democracy. (3) Then there must be the humanities, consisting of courses geared to give the student a sense of morality and a set of values. These values, incidentally, are democratic values, established by society. (4) Meanwhile, certain areas that don't quite fit into these three categories are subject to debate. For example, is history a social science or a "humanity"? There is less question, of course, about what history lessons should do; they are to show how civilization is on the way from an abominably primitive stage to a golden future of a warless, harmonious, perfectly democratic society.

Dualism Again

Observe now how this type of curriculum has in structure and in content been adopted and adapted by Christian dualistic schools. The three divisions established by secular education remain basically unchanged. (1) The natural sciences by and large still examine simply a world of matter run by inherent natural law — except, of course, that this world of nature was created by God and is in some undefined way subject to his providence. (2) The social studies are taught in very much the same way as in the secular school, with stress on the ideal of American democracy as a way of life. The autonomous rational dignity of man, meanwhile, has been replaced somewhat by the concept of man made in the image of God. (3) The

100

humanities continue to be designed to give the student a set of values and virtues. Often these virtues differ very little from those taught in the secular schools – the dignity of man, the need for honesty, punctuality, diligence, tolerance, patience, citizenship, etc. Added to the humanities section are the Bible courses, designed to give the pupil an added spiritual dimension. (4) History as well is commonly taught in Christian schools in very much the same way as in the secular school. Not that the Christian history teacher blatantly teaches that man will reach a golden future. He substitutes the concept of the "plan of God" for that idea, and that is good. At the same time, however, the understanding of the actual historical process itself remains very much the same as that of the secular history teacher. That historical process continues to be seen as a chain of events occurring in the context of cause and effect. As a result, often in history class the student learns no more than (a) the dates, (b) the causes, and (c) the results of historical events. Thus often the "plan of God" concept no more than baptizes what I believe to be an inherently secular understanding of historical events.

The Effects of Individualism

This dualism has been aggravated by individualism. What is individualism? It is a view of man that goes way back to the ancient pagan Greeks. It is the idea that men are really only individual islands, and that each is on his own. They must cooperate, of course, but only because of necessity. The ideal man is the individual, independent man, who stands on his own two feet. In North America individualism found fertile soil. Who doesn't know of the ideal of rugged American individualism?

The Christian school curriculum, in imitation of that of the secular school, is too often geared to train the Christian pupil to be an individual who must take his individual place in society. In dualistic fashion a Christian element is added to this training by saying that the individual station which the graduate must occupy is the spot where God has placed him, where — in addition to simply doing his daily work — he must witness to other individuals. This witness is to be accomplished first of all by word of mouth, that is, by explaining that Christ saves one's soul, or by inviting fellow workers to church; and secondly by model Christian behavior, that is, by personal virtues such as honesty and punctuality. This may be acceptable as far as it goes. How the Christian religion, however, actually relates to the *work* the individual is doing is little understood beyond a vague notion of doing it all to the glory of God. Similarly, how the Christian community should corporately come to expression as the Body of Christ in areas other than the institutional church is a greatly ignored question in much of Christian education. Indeed, our Christian schools are no strangers to the spirit of individualism!

The Biblical Kingdom Vision

To get at a Christian curriculum, we must recognize this state of affairs, and begin to counteract its effects by means of substituting a full-orbed biblical Kingdom vision. Such a full-orbed vision will be antithetical to the dualism and individualsim now commonly perpetuated under the cloak of Christianity. A biblical Kingdom vision, I am sure, will lead toward the establishment and development of an *integral* (as opposed to *dualistic*) Christian curriculum and education.

In essence the biblical Kingdom vision hinges on three focus points; namely, (1) who God is, (2) who man is, and (3) what the world is.

(1) *Who God is:* God is not some distant being in whose eternal mind a blueprint can be found according to

which all events and all things are patterned. Rather, God is Jehovah, the Creator of heaven and earth, who speaks his *Word* to the world, so that all things, men and birds and rivers and mountains *respond* to that Word. "By the Word of his mouth were the heavens made and all the hosts of them by the breath of his mouth" the Psalmist sings in Psalm 33. And Psalm 148 urges "Praise Jehovah from the earth, ye sea monsters and all deeps; fire and hail, snow and vapor, stormy wind, *fulfilling his Word.*"

(2) *Who man is:* man is the crown of creation, made to represent the Lord in dominion over the earth. Sin brought about the great divide of mankind into (a) disobedient apostasy, and (b) a principially obedient Kingdom community called to carry on the reconciling work of Jesus Christ, under whose feet all things have been subjected.

(3) *What the world is:* the world is not an aggregate of molecules and atoms functioning according to some inherent natural law which God observes from some great distance as an impartial bystander. The world, which has been called into existence by God's Word, is at this very moment still being maintained and upheld by that same Word of power. For the curriculum it is of the utmost importance that we understand this scriptural revelation. Things, plants, animals, men, the whole universe; everything is what it is because it is upheld and structured by God's Word, that is, by God's commands and ordinances. "By the Word of his power," we read in Hebrews 1:3, "all things are upheld." (See also Genesis 1, Psalm 104, 119, Job 38, etc.)

From the very beginning the curriculum in the Christian school must be designed to provide and implement the biblical Kingdom context for every pupil. From the very earliest grades our children must be taught to understand God's world as the home for men, in which men are called to carry out the Lord's bidding, from which men because of sin have become alienated. From the earliest grades our children must be taught to understand that to be a Christian is not just to be an American citizen like any other American with some church-going and personal witnessing attached; but rather, that to be a Christian means to be a member of the communion of the saints, called out from those who reject the Lord, called to do the Lord's will everywhere, never merely as so many loose, unrelated individuals — that's that individualism again! — but always as members of the one body of Christ, each with his own function, yes, but never a function apart from all the other members.

You begin to sense, then, the immense task of designing a Christian school curriculum in accordance with the biblical Kingdom vision — geared to train Kingdom citizens. That's the heart of the matter, you see. Our Chrisitan school graduates must not be *merely* clean-living, upright, and honest individuals. They must be more than that. They must be Christians who understand what their corporate task is as agents of the reconciliation of Jesus Christ, and how to go about that task in an apostate, God-ignoring, and hell-bound civilization.

The Kingdom Vision Affects the Christian School Curriculum

How, concretely now, does this Kingdom vision and task affect the curriculum? Here are just a few examples. First, the natural sciences cannot be taught as a mere body of knowledge which explains the universe as a cold world of matter, atoms, and inherent natural laws. Rather, natural science must explain the created order as structured and responding to God's Word of power. The effects of the concept of inherent natural law must be radically eliminated, a most difficult thing to do.[1] Natural science, moreover, must be designed to give the child an understanding of the creation of God as the home for men, which must be unfolded in the name of the Lord. Natural science, therefore, as well as technology, must be understood as a *cultural* activity, as an obedient or disobedient response to the will of the Lord. I might add, at this point, that Christian elementary schools often succeed much more in conveying the biblical concept of God's world to the children than the advanced levels of education. Much of this success, in fact, is rendered meaningless in junior high, high school, and college, where natural sciences once more are treated as so many independent and unrelated bodies of abstract facts.

Second, social sciences can no longer be taught as mere descriptions of what is actually taking place. Rather, the God-oriented norms and ordinances for the various societal structures such as state, family, marriage, school, labor, and industry must be clarified to the Christian student, so that in terms of these norms he will gain insight into the *de*formations that have taken place in our civilization. This, in turn, will enable him to join the throng of fellow-believers as a Kingdom citizen, struggling together with them for the *re*formation of what unbelief has distorted.

Third, "humanities" can no longer be courses whose function it is to instill a set of values and a sense of morality in pupils. "Humanities" will no longer be contrasted with natural sciences as value is contrasted with fact, since natural sciences themselves, as I indicated a moment ago, must be understood as cultural activity, and therefore as a response to what the Lord wants men to do. The Kingdom vision must guide again: how has the art, music, language and literature of civilization been deformed by men who turned their backs on the Lord? How can we understand the nature of art and language and all the other fields so that these dimensions of God's world, too, can be reclaimed for Jesus Christ? Take art, for example. Day after day the Christian community is bombarded by the secular spirits in art, on TV, in magazines, on the billboards along the highway. All of this molds and forms us, and shapes us into the standard American consumer. Where is the Christian alternative? The Christian curriculum, therefore, must incorporate work in art in such a way that Kingdom citizens come out of our schools ready and able to do battle with the spirits, including those spirits that have gained control of the art forms of North America.

Fourth, history courses can no longer be taught as masses of events related in a context of cause and effect. Rather, history will be seen as man's response to God's call to be active in the world, to keep and to dress the garden. The various sequences of events, therefore, must be evaluated in terms of a biblically-directed understanding of God's will for cultural development. History courses must vividly highlight the antithesis between the children of light and the children of darkness. Historical studies must equip the Christian school graduate to understand the spirits of the age, their nature, their origin, and their effectiveness. In this way the Christian school graduate can take his place in the army of the Lord to combat the forces of secularism, humanism, pragmatism, dualism, individualism, and all other isms that are not of God and which now collectively have a death grip on North American education, politics, economics, art, and communications.

Fundamental Issue Number Two: Encyclopedia

But wait a minute, you may say at this point, just one moment! Didn't you say earlier that the division of the curriculum into natural science, social science, and humanities is simply an adaptation of secular curriculum patterns? Aren't you yourself using these categories now?

Building a Curriculum with the Kingdom Vision

To get at this, we need to raise the second fundamental issue. It is this; What understanding of the encyclopedia does the curriculum presuppose? By encyclopedia I simply mean the way in which human knowledge is divided into various branches. Encyclopedia refers to the relationship among the sciences and disciplines. Here I want to emphatically assert that one's understanding and analysis of the encyclopedia is determined by one's philosophical position.

The problem of the encyclopedia already confronted pagan scholars in ancient times. Aristotle, for example, divided the various branches of knowledge of that time into two categories, the theoretical and the practical sciences, with logic as a tool to be used in both. in the Middle Ages the curriculum was divided into the seven liberal arts; namely, the *trivium,* composed of grammar, rhetoric, and dialectic; and the *quadrivium,* which contained arithmetic, geometry, music, and astronomy.

The Origin of Present Curricular Division

In our own times the standard division of subject matter into natural sciences, social sciences, and humanities is a reflection of a modern philosophical – non-Christian – view of reality. It arises out of a conception which holds that the world of autonomous matter and natural law confronts the free thinking, creating human agent. During the first three hundred years of the modern era, that is, from the fifteenth to the eighteenth centuries, scholars greatly emphasized mathematics, physics, and astronomy – the so-called natural sciences. The universe was believed to be like a machine, capable of being rationally understood and controlled by means of the natural sciences.

In the eighteenth and nineteenth centuries, however, it became recognized that not all of life is a matter of physics and mathematics. Not all the world is a machine. *Human values and feelings constitute a different field of investigation.* This realization reemphasized the study of the so-called "humanities," that is, the study of human life and values. At this time the so-called social and behavioral sciences began to develop as a further reaction to the one-sided stress on natural science. The classic formulation of this situation was given by such nineteenth century scholars as Dilthey, Windelband, and Rickert, who divided the encyclopedia into *Naturwissenschaften* (science of nature) and *Geisteswissenschaften* (sciences of the "mind"). This, in brief and summary fashion, is the background of much of our curriculum today.

These nineteenth-century formulations, in spite of their presupposed non-Christian world view, nevertheless exhibit traces of truth. All these men, although rejecting the light of the Scriptures, nevertheless were active in *God's* creation. They were actively investigating and analyzing the various states of affairs which are structured by *God's ordinances.* Because of their darkened hearts and minds, however, their understanding of God's creation and their formulations of its meaning became radically distorted. Instead of seeing that the diversity of the creation was upheld by the unifying power of God's Word, they began to interpret the handiwork of the Lord as "nature" — a nature run according to inherent physical and mathematical laws. And instead of seeing man as God's creature, mandated to take care of all that the Lord had made, they interpreted human life to be a rational autonomous product of an evolutionary process. Man, as a biological organism equipped with a rational mind, must order his society according to certain basic needs and democratic ideals, if he is to survive in an intrinsically hostile world. Thus the contrast between the "humanities" and the natural sciences is rooted in the supposed contrast between man and a cold world of "nature." The social and behavioral sciences, meanwhile, are seen as providing the link between the two poles of man and nature.

The Result of These Non-Christian Formulations of the Encyclopedia

Note, by the way, the results of this darkened and distorted understanding of the created order. Modern man in rejecting the Word of God thereby rejected the very principle of unity that holds the encyclopedia together. In Jesus Christ, remember, all things cohere. (See Ephesians 1 and Colossians 1.) Without Jesus Christ that coherence is gone. What is left is fragmentation, leaving in turn a fragmented curriculum. Hence the student walks from one class to another without having any idea how the various courses and subjects are related. Somehow the student is expected to develop by means of the "educational experience" to be had in each class. Experience of this kind, however, leads to nothing but utter frustration. Life is of one piece because the creation of God is of one piece, and when the curriculum doesn't reflect that, there is nothing but irrelevance. Much of the student revolt of the last decade is due to that irrelevance. You see, the loss of the understanding that the creation of God is structured by His Word and ordinances and upheld moment by moment through Jesus Christ means that the very *meaning* of the world and of life is removed. Consequently the irrelevance of the secular school curriculum leads to ever greater meaninglessness. No wonder that the late sixties drug culture, the hippies, and others became such a prevalent phenomenon in the early seventies. Their protest was not merely directed against a greedy capitalistic society, but to the utter meaninglessness of North American education as well. No wonder that so many turn to astrology, Zen Buddhism, and the occult in the desperate quest for *meaning*. What a task we have as

John Van Dyk

Christian educational institutions to restore *meaning* to the curriculum, and thus restoring meaning to the entire educational enterprise, and bringing the healing vision of God's Word and power through Jesus Christ to American education.

The Christian school curriculum, let us admit, has not escaped this kind of fragmentation and meaninglessness. In our Christian schools, too, many students have no idea of how their course work is interrelated, and what it means for their Christian life. The dualism is so clear again. Add to this once more the pernicious influence of individualism, and you understand why so often Christian education is carried on by teachers who work as isolated entities in isolated classrooms. Often the teacher in Room 201 has no idea of what the teacher in Room 202 is doing. That such a state of affairs handicaps the development of a unified, meaningful, coherent and consistent curriculum is evident to everyone.

How to Counteract Fragmentation

To begin developing such a consistent program of studies we need to learn to understand much more fully what forces have shaped the present curricular pattern of encyclopedia, and also to learn to communally utilize philosophical tools which will enable us to construct an understanding of the encyclopedia which is in accord with the biblical Kingdom vision I referred to earlier.

The Institute for Christian Studies in Toronto is therefore no idle venture. We need the foundational studies in order to gain some perspective on the nature and history of the curriculum. The ICS needs to be supported by finances and prayer. It needs the involvement of a much larger segment of the Christian community in North America. Much more cooperation and coordination are needed in the effort to learn to understand what we are up against in curriculum construction.

What about philosophical tools? By philosophical tools I mean a systematic, biblically worked-out understanding of the structure and interrelatedness of all that the Lord has created and upholds. It is the specific task of a systematic Christian philosophy, I believe, to articulate that interrelatedness, so that the coherence of the various sciences and disciplines can become visible.

Often it is said that we don't need such a philosophy, for we have the Bible. The Bible however, does not tell us how sociology differs from anthropology, no more than it tells us how to calculate square roots of whole numbers. These are tasks that *we* must do, in obedience to God's command to develop and unfold, always in the light of the Scriptures.

The Philosophy of the Cosmonomic Idea as an Effective Tool

Is there such an articulated systematic Christian philosophy available? I do not hesitate to state that I have found the Philosophy of the Cosmonomic Idea extremely helpful in gaining an understanding of the coherence of the creation order and therefore of the encyclopedia as well. This philosophical system, utilized by a growing number of teachers and students around the world, is built on the biblical world views of Augustine, Calvin, and Abraham Kuyper, and was developed by a group of men of whom such scholars as Herman Dooyeweerd, D.H. Th. Vollenhoven, and H.G. Stoker are perhaps the best known.

The Philosophy of the Cosmonomic Idea is a tool, not a creed. It is a servant, not a master. It needs constant discussion, revision, and improvement. But already it is capable of offering us a framework in which to cast the entire encyclopedia of the sciences and the structure of the curriculum in a meaningful, coherent way.[2]

The Philosophy of the Cosmonomic Idea takes its starting point from the biblical given that the entire created order is subject to God's will, laws, and ordinances. It then works out this biblical given into a tentative systematic understanding of how the created order functions in response to the structuring, ordering Word of God. This systematic elaboration is carried out in a conscious and prayerful attempt to constantly listen to what Scripture tells us about God's cosmos as a whole. The Scriptures give us the outlines and the contours, so to speak, in which we can begin to fit the pieces.

How will an implementation of a systematic understanding of the creation order affect the curriculum in our schools?

First of all, it will immediately reverse the present trend toward increasing fragmentation. It will make it possible somewhere along the line for the Christian student to realize that going from math class to literature class is not the same thing as going from one world to another. Christian education will become a process whereby our children and young people take hold of God's coherent creation as it consists in Jesus Christ. A curriculum so conceived and constructed accordingly can indeed be the integrating guideline in Christian education, because it will be able to implement a *meaningful* education.

In the second place, a systematic understanding of the encyclopedia will enable the staff of the Christian school to develop as a team. The teacher in Room 201 *will* know what the teacher in Room 202 is doing because they will have been able to communicate with each other *within the same framework.* Both are involved in different aspects of *one* task, which is now *academically* understood as well. The implications of this point are many. Team teaching will take on new meaning. The interchange of syllabi and class notes will take on new meaning. Faculty meetings and Parent/Teacher Association meetings will take on a renewed color.

In the third place, a systematic understanding of the encyclopedia allows for a meaningful core curriculum as well as meaningful majors and minors that don't drift away into isolated irrelevant specialization. All course work can now be integrated and unified.

An additional advantage of the Philosophy of the Cosmonomic Idea is that it affords us the opportunity to evaluate non-Christian world views more critically and more accurately. This means, in effect, that it enables us to evaluate the various types of curricula more accurately. The whole point is that there is no curriculum which does not have a philosophy, a world view behind it. All curriculum construction takes place against the background of some form of an encyclopedia, chaotic, disorganized, or unformulated as such an encyclopedia may be. To recognize this is a prerequisite to the construction of a Christian curriculum. Those who claim that there is very little relationship among the sciences and disciplines and subject matters, and that the encyclopedia involves an irrelevant question anyway, are in deep trouble — on which grounds do they decide what to include in and what to exclude from the curriculum?

Conclusion

How do we go from here? The next step would involve the arrangement of subject matter into a meaningful consistent program of studies, able to lead the child all the way from grade school through college. In this way the curriculum can be fleshed out and concretized so that it can indeed function as the guideline for Christian education.

Already much developmental curricular work has been

done. During the summers of 1971 and 1972, for example, the Association for the Advancement of Christian Scholarship (AACS) conducted workshops in which teachers came together in Toronto to work out, under the guidance of Dr. Arnold DeGraaff, detailed courses of study for the various grades. Very promising and helpful results have already become available, especially in the areas of social studies, Bible, history and mathematics. Meanwhile, as we make progress in this way, the parallel development of a Christian theory of pedagogy and child development must be worked out. Then we shall be on the way toward a really integral Christian school curriculum.

What an immense task awaits us. What a responsibility we have. But what an exciting venture for all of us as Kingdom citizens – to construct a truly Christian curriculum to implement a truly Christian education.

We need to join hands in this venture, as Christian brothers and sisters in the Lord, as the communion of the saints. That will require humility on the part of all of us, and love, and patience, but also courage and boldness. In it all we *have* the unity and bond of faith in Jesus Christ, who is also Lord of the curriculum.

We live in a dark and confused world, a world which has lost the way. We as the children of light have Jesus Christ, who *is* the Way. Shall we not stand together, struggle together, and help each other? Shall we not work together, led by the Spirit of God and equipped with the power of the Lord, so that his Name will be magnified in the twentieth century world of education?

May the Lord bless us so that even the *curriculum* of our schools will be like a strong light, a signpost of the Kingdom, a powerful witness in a dark and confused world.

Building a Curriculum with the Kingdom Vision

Footnotes

[1]In a typical dualistic Christian school, natural science courses limit God's involvement with the world to two parts. First, God created it all; and second, God is sovereign over it all and takes care of it all. This is good, of course, but it doesn't go far enough. In fact, usually, after these two things have been said, the question of God's relation to the world doesn't come up again. The great danger is then that the various theories of inherent natural law take over again, placing us right back in a secular framework of reference. It is necessary to eliminate the theories of natural law, and to begin to understand and analyze all functioning in the cosmos as a response to God's structurating law.

[2]More information about the Philosophy of the Cosmonomic Idea can be obtained by reading *In the Twilight of Western Thought* or *A New Critique of Theoretical Thought* by Herman Dooyeweerd. Both of these books and other literature from the same integrally Christian perspective are available from Tomorrow's Book Club, 229 College St. West, Toronto M5T 1R4, Ontario, Canada.

4

ORGANIZING THE SCHOOL FOR LEARNING

Schools are for Learning

by Adrian Peetoom

Schools are not places for teaching, they are places for learning. That is, those who are responsible for the organization of schools — and in a Christian community all its supporters are — must make all decisions in the light of how their actions influence *learning* in the school.

If we are agreed on this much, then the rest of this essay will be an exploration of what we can do together to make schools better places for learning. . .and places for better learning.

When we think of learning in the school, we must ask ourselves some questions about who the learners are, and what kind of people make it possible for learning to occur. We want to know something about the nature of children — who they are and how they learn. Then it should be quite clear that the way we organize schools must be in harmony with what we discover about who children are and how they learn.

So our first task is set. What do we know about our children?

The Christian Way of Life

Christian schools are part of the faith activity of the Christian community. The Christian community must never lose sight of the fact that it is a confessional community, a community of believers in Jesus Christ. Believers are confessors. It is in character with the community nature of the discovery program, that we first confess together what the scriptures teach us about our children.

Our children are part of mankind. Mankind was created in the image of God, given a task to develop and build creation. In Adam our children are part of that being created in the image of God, part of the task force which God established to bring his marvelous creation to full flower.

But in Adam too our children fell into sin, said NO! to the rule of God and YES! to the rule of their own hearts, and disqualified themselves from further service to the God of creation.

In Adam too, however, our children are part of a mankind given a second chance in Jesus Christ. In Jesus' victory on the cross they are restored to their office as builders and developers of God's marvelous creation. Children too are still faced with the effects of sin, with brokenness of life and childhood. But in Jesus Christ they may go to work again in the knowledge that the ultimate victory is assured, and that while the works of mankind will not stand forever, the works of Jesus Christ (through mankind) will. That is, all men, adults and children have an office of developing life in such a way that the results of their work stand out as clear signposts pointing the way to the second coming of Jesus Christ, when sin and its effects will be destroyed for good.

In that faith we are a Christian community, and in that faith we organize our personal concerns, families, churches, schools, politics, art so that in all these aspects of life we give expression to our confession. We do not hide this Good News, on the contrary, we set this light on a hill so that it can be seen for miles around. We proclaim in the way we educate our children that Jesus Christ has made it possible again to do it right.

And we confess we have only the beginnings of such an obedience, a mustard seed – but it grows into a big tree; it's a stammering confession––but it will move mountains.

But thus far our confession has only affirmed that children are part of mankind, that children are men. In order to come to grips with children's learning in schools we must listen to what God has to say about children, specifically. For if it is true that creation is God's work, and that his law holds for it all, it holds for childhood too. In other words the question must be asked whether childhood is just a stage on the way to becoming an adult, or whether it has its own unique place, and if you will, laws.

In history this question has been answered mostly in a way which did not leave children to be children, but considered them only adults in the making. That was to be expected. In Abraham's time, and later in biblical times too, children were very quickly fitted into the nomadic and agricultural patterns of life. As soon as children could move about on their own they would be given small tasks in the overall life of the family, tribe and nation. Even today small children quickly take part in their parents' work on so-called family farms.

One reason for this was the enormously hard struggle for mere survival. Israel may have been a land of milk and honey, but any even superficial study of the history and geography of that part of the world will show that the honey did not just come dripping into Israelites' tongues, and the milk came in small quantities, from goats and sheep, and I understand that both these animals are more cantankerous than the truly domesticated cows of our time, Israelites had to work hard. "Give us this day our daily bread" becomes a prayer loaded with immediate meaning, when even in Jesus' time almost all people were

121

workers by the day (remember the parable Jesus tells about such people) and the bread for that day had to be earned that day.

In fact, this condition of hard work and the conditions in which payment — or lack of it — was a day-to-day affair made it very natural that there was little opportunity for childhood, little other possibility but to consider the purpose of parenthood and education to be the making of people who are quickly economically self-sufficient. The quicker children can look after the animals and crops, the quicker they lessen the burden on the rest of the family and tribe. The success of bringing up children is measured by how quickly these children become adults.

There is another fact to be considered. We have grown accustomed to a very small infant mortality rate. It is rare for a baby to die, and it is considered a great tragedy. But under the more primitive living conditions of peoples before us, until quite recently, infant mortality was very high indeed; sixty, seventy percent or even higher. Just read the history books and notice how large the families were of important figures and how only a few of those children grew into adults. Proper nutrition and hygiene are very modern concepts, but they, more than even medical research are responsible for the almost one-hundred percent survival rate of babies and small children.

But what is important for us to remember is how this affected the way adults thought of children. If you lived as parents with the knowledge that probably most of your children would die, you would be somewhat less enthusiastic about them when they are very young, for they could be taken away at a moment's notice. You would guard yourself against loving them too much too soon, not deliberately, but unconsciously. And it is obvious from the historical record, from literature, from poetry and folk songs, that people in former days were much more matter-of-fact about their children, less "emotionally involved" as we would call it today. They accepted as part of life that most of their children would die.

Even today there is a saying in India that "it is sometimes said that the loss of a child s a great sorrow, but the loss of a bullock is a calamity." I think it is fair to say that when the Israelites praised God for their children, they would do that not thinking about babies and very young children, but about children of an age that they knew meant a good chance for survival.

We get some glimpse of that in Psalms 127 and 128. Under the conditions we have discussed we begin to grasp the full depth of meaning of a psalmist who says:

> Sons are a bounty from Yahweh
> he rewards with descendants;
> like the arrows in a hero's hand
> are the sons you father when young.
> Happy the man who has filled his quiver
> with arrows of this sort;
> in dispute with his enemies at the gate,
> he will not be worsted. (Psalm 127)

A quiver full, I'm told, is six. If we consider too that one of the most prized literary techniques of Hebrew writers was the deliberate exaggeration (we call it hyperbole), we can sense that the psalmist here is talking about something which would not happen every day, but which, when it did happen, should be seen as the miraculous work of Yahweh. In Psalm 128 the same thing is said in a different way.

> 'Your wife, a fruitful vine
> on the inner walls of your house
> Your sons: round your table
> like shoots around an olive tree.'

In other words, your wife was fruitful enough to have many children, and your children were strong enough to survive until such time that they were old enough to sit around your table.

Conditions of low infant survival and the necessary very hard, physical work of people lasted until quite recently. And parallel with it, the view that children were only adults in the making.

But we live in a different era now.

Today almost all children grow up to be adults. And at the same time it is far less necessary for young people to enter the labour force quickly. That means that there is more opportunity for children to remain children longer, and children have grasped that opportunity. Adults have become aware of this, and you will often find a reporter describing children who have been through much poverty and deprivation — children in Northern Ireland, Viet Nam, the slums of large cities — as children with "old eyes," meaning adult eyes. Those reporters have caught on to the fact that when children have to live adult lives too soon, they will be destroyed as children.

Another illustration of children remaining children longer is the fact that we now recognize a stage in life called "teenager." Before there were only children increasing their involvement in the adult world each year until about age thirteen or fourteen. Then they would marry and be adults. But as it became less necessary to involve all children immediately in the production process and other facets of adult life, room was created for an intermediate stage between childhood and adulthood. We call it "being a teenager." It is an age after childhood, but before the demands of adulthood. And today we are finding that there is another discernible stage between being a teenager and an adult, the stage of what we might call being a "youth." That is, a person whose mind and body are probably ready to undertake the responsibilities of adulthood, but who needs more time — for various reasons — before he is ready to undertake those responsibilities.

I might say in passing that the same kind of development has taken place at the other side of the age spectrum. Just as there were few children, so there have always been few old people. The same conditions have created larger numbers of older people, who are not just adults — in the prime of cultural participation so to speak — but a group of people with capacities and needs all their own.

Now what does this all mean in biblical terms? How does this all fit in with our earlier confession about man, created in the image of God, in the vineyard of God's creation and with the task of developing creation and having dominion over it? It means simply this, that under God's rule the earth *has* been developed, and that man *has* found and is finding more treasures in that creation all the time. God's history is man doing his job, as God's viceregent. That job *is* going on, even if people do not acknowledge God's reign, for Jesus Christ *has* gained the final victory and *is* sitting at the right hand of God the Father, ruling creation through His Body, His People and using even the work of unbelievers for His own purposes. To gain time away from the elementary task of providing daily bread is a blessing of God, potentially available in the beginning, but brought about through man's work on earth. So is a larger population, better health, more of what we wrongly call "leisure time." So is an opportunity to be a baby, a child, a teenager, a youth, an adult and a senior citizen. The unfolding of creation — unstoppable, for it is God's intent — has become particularly evident in our time as undreamed of opportunities for service have become visible.

Only, we have to learn how to use these opportunities. What is particularly important for us is to acknowledge that there is more to being a child than merely being an adult in formation, and to confess that the fact that we have learned this much is a blessing of the Lord, and an opportunity for further service and praise to our Maker.

The Office of Children

Let's look at children with new eyes, for this is our task.

To me the most vivid picture of a child learning is the one with a little baby lying on its back in mother's lap and staring up to mother who is talking to it. I have often watched such a scene, and somehow was gripped by a realization that a child's learning was going on here in the most intense way possible. The baby's head exudes learning, even the back of its head seems involved in it. It is the most elementary and yet perhaps the most penetrating learning moment available to us. Just a mother talking to her little baby.

The mother is not thinking about education, while she's doing it. She is just loving that baby, in a way that has made sense throughout the generations. But the act of love is made up of many elements.

1. It is an act of love which needs a physical touch. The baby is closely held, usually the back of its head resting on the mother's knees, or its head in the mother's hand. There is a physical belonging together.

2. It is an act of love which needs language. No one knows how much of language very young babies already "understand," but we do know that without many such experiences at a very young age, children's language development will be retarded. We must also notice that the mother's language during this period is a very unique one. It is usually very "sound" oriented, that is, it has a musical, chanting quality, and the particular words are not chosen for specific logical meanings. Rather there is a lot of repetition, and usually a chanting retelling of what

mother has just finished doing for that baby, or about what is going on at that moment, or about what other children or Dad have done or are doing. It is a very private world between mother and child.

3. There are other elements involved, for instance the physical well-being of both mother and child, a surrounding home of love, opportunity and time to do it, in short the surrounding of a rich and loving family.

However, the most important conclusion we may draw from it is that the experienced adult creates an environment totally suited to the child, one at that child's level – social, intellectual, emotional. And precisely because of _that_ – because of the being at its own level – learning occurs. It is the experienced adult who creates that just perfect environment, truly a child's world, and it is precisely then that learning occurs.

You do not forever talk and act this way with your children. This particular act is soon replaced with other acts. For instance, a baby at five months is moving around more, and before too long Dad comes home from work, takes that baby on his knee, and with his own hands safely around the baby's upper body, bounces it up and down, talking to it in less gentle ways, more boisterous. And again specialists in the field tell us, that if this kind of thing does not occur at the right time, learning is retarded.

It is not necessary to follow child development in detail. It is sufficient to observe that good families are good families precisely because in their home environments are provided in which the child can find the experience right for his age and right for his developments, and in which that child is able to respond freely. And when that happens, children learn a lot, and the right things.

Schools are not families. But neither is learning limited to the schools. All of us, children and adults alike, learn all the time in the very environments in which we find

Adrian Peetoom

ourselves. The uniqueness of the school lies in the fact that it is an environment created specifically for learning, learning is the purpose for which it is established. But it is a child who goes to school, and it is that child who can learn only when he finds himself in an environment which is right for him, in which he finds the circumstances, conditions, and also the materials which fit into his world, and belong to it. *This is the principle for organizing the school for learning. Organizing the school for learning is simply creating a child's proper environment, and the learning will take care of itself.*

A Difficult Task

But this is probably very difficult to do for a number of reasons.

1. The first of these reasons is that not all that much is known about the learning process itself. It is only in recent times that research into the nature of learning has started. Most educational research has busied itself with the nature of teaching, not learning, and it now looks very much as if a lot of effort and money has been wasted on it. In fact, from studies and reports it has become clear that students are not learning any better or faster, in spite of the following changes wrought in the last 20 years:

teachers are trained better and longer
better and more varied books and other learning materials are available
more money is spent
schooling lasts longer
schooling is more varied
more types of schools are available
better school buildings have been built

Anyone interested in pursuing these rather startling facts should read Charles Silberman's *Crisis in the Classroom.*

128

The problem has been that most of these efforts were dedicated to the principle that a child is simply an adult in the making, and the improvements in education were attempts to get a child to become an adult quicker than before. This view was a mistake, and it should surprise no one that the educational schemes built on this wrong were like houses built on sand.

What is needed then is more learning about the learning process. We need to know much more about "levels" and "stages of development." And we have to train teachers to become much more discerning about whether children are learning, and when. We must get away from assuming that learning occurs just because we feel very confident about the quality of teaching. For what we understand to be quality of teaching, is the putting into more simple and childish terms the things we as adults know and respond to. But we must become concerned about the child's unique experiences of the world in which he lives. I want to put it in very vivid terms. Children are always learning, for they are human and humans are always learning. The question is: *What is being learned?*

And when we think of the prototype classroom, with forty students seated neatly in rows, quiet, each having the same book, and a teacher in front of those rows, talking most of the time, occasionally asking questions intended mostly to check whether kids pay attention, then students are learning quite a bit. They are learning that school is a terrible place; where you survive best when you keep your mouth shut, where you learn how to answer the teacher in such a way that *he* is satisfied; where you can't talk to anybody; where you have no choice over what you want to do, or when, and where you learn to hide your real feelings so as not to get punished by your teacher, principal and parents; where you survive mostly because at least recess is not too far away. Schools are work, and learning is work, and the opposite of work is play. That's what children learn in such schools.

I have exaggerated the case on purpose. . .but not much. There are such rooms, plenty of them. This is not because teachers are evil, or even unwilling, nor because they hate kids. It is because those teachers have been brought up themselves in classrooms which taught them that no child enjoys learning, and that you better be firm and strict, for it is the nature of the child to not want to learn. After all, there's such a thing as total depravity, isn't there? Well then, what else do you expect teachers to do?

Luckily most classrooms are less sterile than the one I have described to you, particularly with the current abundance of educational materials readily available. But how often even in those potentially learning-rich classrooms does a teacher prevent the materials and the students from getting together? Sometimes for learning to occur, it would be necessary for the teacher to step out of the way. for the teacher to step out of the way.

2. The second reason why it will be very difficult to organize the classroom for real learning is that we have been doing it the old way for so long that most of our structures and ways of educating are reflections of children as adults in the making. When in a real sense children are looked upon only as adults but not yet, knowledge tends to be thought of as the property of adults. The teacher becomes the container of that knowledge, the package of it so to speak, and so does the textbook, and together, textbook and teacher, they transmit that knowledge to the child, and when the child has learned *it* he has learned. So runs our presumption. Textbooks get written that way, teachers' notes are organized that way, there are lesson plans — so much time for the math box, so much time for the reading box, so much time for the social studies box — and the schools are built like boxes too. In other words, curriculum, school organization, methodology, teacher

training, parents' expectations, testing, reporting, evaluating, and finally the whole reward system (pass the right exam and we'll give you the right job) are all built on a foundation which we have already rejected as basically not in keeping with God's created order. To change all this is no easy task. Blowing up the schools is no remedy, mostly because we would have to build new schools again. Firing the teachers won't help either, for their replacements have been trained in the same way. The worst of it all is that for most children it is already too late to change. They have already been spoiled for real intense school learning. I know of high schools that began to offer learning freedom to their students only to find that the students did not want this freedom, for it paralyzed them and frightened them.

So we must begin to recognize that we cannot change the situation overnight, and that very realistically we must begin our process of educational reformation from where we are now.

I do not want to plead for something however. It is in the nature of our situation that there will arise an increasing number of alternative projects to our Christian schools, right within that Christian community. Some frustrated teachers are going to open a "free school" and invite kids to come to them, and they won't wait until there is a properly constituted Christian school society. Others, parents and teachers, will take their children out of school completely, and create within their own homes environments for learning. I beg you to recognize these attempts for what they are; namely the inevitable consequences of frustration over reform which is slow, or not forthcoming at all, and honest attempts at finding alternatives. If it happens in your community – and it has already happened in mine – don't blame the people who are doing it, blame yourself and the community which made it happen. And keep contact with these people, for they will experience much pain which we can avoid if we're smart. For new kinds of schooling are inevitable, even and perhaps especially within the Christian community.

How Children Learn

We have seen that if we wish to structure education as a place for learning, we will have a difficult task. Difficult, but I believe not impossible. That too is part of our confession, that we shall never be given impossible tasks, only beautiful ones.

We do know enough about children already to make a good start.

1. *We know that all children love learning.* Just check with kindergarten and first grade teachers and they will tell you that all children are eager learners. *All* children, that is, who have had a "normal" home, and who are in good health. It is rare in the early grades to hear educators talk about "lazy" children, or "dumb" children. It is in the early grades that experienced teachers can easily pinpoint what kind of homes their students come from, for their experience has taught them that it is normal to expect these youngsters to be brightly intense about learning. And as school has not had time to dull the brightness, only their students' previous experience can account for "abnormality."

2. *We know that young children are playful, and we have discovered that for young children play* is *learning.* For even very young children the seemingly erratic behavior of hands groping for each other, then finding each other, of hands seemingly at random groping around until other objects are touched — the kind of thing that has had many a parent enthralled for hours — is in reality a learning of what it is that surrounds the baby. And what are natural toys for young toddlers? Boxes, and blocks,

and stones, and balls, and bells. What is so remarkable about those? They are the shapes of life, for they come in all shapes, and textures, and weights and measures, and sounds. You don't *teach* a child that a stone is hard, he play-learns it. You don't *teach* a child that a small block will always go on a big block, but the other way around is tricky – he play-learns it.

3. *We know that children learn at different speeds.* This is so obvious that it needs no elaboration.

4. *We know that a child does not learn everything at the same speed.* This is not quite so obvious, and only recently have educators begun to treat this discovery seriously.

5. *We know that children do not learn at the same speed at all times.* Experienced parents know that often a child spends months trying to tie knots in his shoelaces, and he does not seem to make much progress. Then one day a father will look at a mother and say, "Hey, John tied his shoelaces." And mother will say, "Come to think of it, he's already been doing it for three weeks." In the meantime John has not thought about the problem since he finally mastered the trick, for it's also true that young children never think much about what they have learned already; they are too busy trying to learn something new. Children's learning in school is not different from their learning at home in this respect.

6. *We know that at certain stages of development the influence of the peer group is the strongest influence of all.* This should come as no surprise to parents of high school children, especially when the subject is "clothes." But so far we have made little educational use of this discovery.

7. *We know that children learn while talking.* It is in their constant verbal reactions to what they experience that they begin to come to grips with the world in which they live, understand it, so to speak; and we know you

cannot learn to talk very well if you don't get a chance to do it very often. For most children talking well results in reading well, writing well and thinking clearly.

8. *We know that children up to the age of puberty learn mostly by doing.* It is only at puberty that children enter an age in which they will be capable of analysis, of abstraction. That is, for most children "theory" is beyond their horizon until after age twelve or thirteen, and even then this ability comes gradually and slowly. Analysis, abstraction, theorizing is the ability to think part of life away from the rest of it, so that by looking at those parts, you get a better understanding of the whole. For instance, a doctor will mentally try to take a kidney out of a patient, and look at it to see whether it is functioning well. If it is not, he may try to cure it. He can only do this mentally, with his mind, but he can do it, and because he can do it, he can find out what's wrong and try to right it.

The point is not that we know adults can do it; the point is that children must grow up first before *they* can. And before they're ready to do it, and learn to do it better, we may not bother them with it.

And the reason that this is so important to remember when we organize the school for learning is that our adult ability to read this material depends to a great extent on our ability to analyze. For when we listen to a lecture or read a piece of non-fiction we constantly think along with the speaker and writer; that is, we constantly accept or reject the problems he raises, and also actively accept or reject the solutions he offers. Children cannot do this in the same manner, and therefore, the lecture method for children is a premature method.

9. *We know that children are very clever in hiding from adults what they have and have not learned.* It is the office of a child to be a learner. Learning is his vocation, his God-given task in life. But as God created man as mankind, as a community of men, so he placed children

with adults. Those adults are to be the children's guides in life. Children do not strike out on their own; on the contrary, they seek the company and guidance and approval of adults, for that is part of their being children.

Blessed are the children when the guidance is biblically correct and rich. But crippled are those children who receive the wrong guidance. When adults are possessed with the wrong vision of life, and when they are insensitive to a child's world, they will offer the wrong guidance. But the child's need remains to respond to that guidance, and in doing so the child will feel his life being distorted. Then the child will rebel, for the vision of life presented to him, and life itself are at war. Yet he will try to keep the adult's approval coming his way; he cannot help himself for he is a child. And therefore the child himself will begin to distort life — to act in ways which are not right.

Children will go to extraordinary lengths to satisfy adults. They will lie, cheat, cause themselves to be punished — all forms of getting attention, and guidance. They will pretend to know, while they do not. They will plead ignorance, while knowing. They will produce behavior expected of them, and at the right times. If adults regard children as evil little monsters, it is as evil little monsters children will behave.

What we observe in schools is that students will study for examinations, only to promptly forget everything they have learned right after the exam. In fact all they have learned is to produce a sufficient number of right answers to escape disapproval. A cartoon illustrates this point very clearly. Two girls stand in front of a classroom, with a note pinned to the door saying, "Today's test postponed." One girl remarks to the other, "We'll have to remember the provincial capitals for another week."

Of course I'm putting my case strongly. I hope that you will not let that bother you. For if you think that my oversimplifications really set up straw men, empty enemies, you are deceiving yourself. Just ask high school teachers about elementary school students; ask college professors about graduates of high schools; ask graduate school deans about undergraduates; ask employers about their new recruits, and you hear one drawn-out wail about "they don't know anything." Just look around you after twenty years of Christian schools in Canada, and ask yourself how many of these graduates are now pillars of wisdom and strength in the Christian community; how many are doing battle on all the fronts of life — there where it counts in the fields of labour, of politics, of economics, of art, of communications, of literature. Worse still, ask the few who do whether they think their schools were responsible.

But there are forces of renewal in education and the Discovery lectures of the AACS are testimony to that. For it is not just when teachers and principals undertake reform that schools will get better. It will take the Christian community to do it, with each segment playing its proper role.

How do we organize a school for learning?

We have learned something already; namely that the question must be rephrased to ask, "How do we organize a school environment so that learning will occur, each child at his appropriate speed, learning the right thing, secure in the knowledge that when he fails he can try again, today, tomorrow or next month? And how do we organize it so that its graduates face the world with competence to judge the spirits whether they be of God? How do we instill the conviction that the task is one of making God-fearing contributions to the world in which we live?

A Guided Tour

This building has doors, but they are open most of the time.

Schools are for *Learning*

In it are learners, most of children's age.

The school buzzes with a hundred conversations at all times.

There are classrooms, but they are often open, and there is a lot of wandering through the halls.

There are a lot of books in that school, and you can find them everywhere.

There are not so many desks as you would expect, and they seem to be arranged every which way.

A lot of kids sit on the floor.

Others stand up.

There is a lot of laughter.

Every corner seems to have junk in it. Lumber. Paint. Glue. Half-finished carpentry.

The walls are almost bent under the weight of paintings, drawings, some skeletons, maps and posters.

From the ceilings hang mobiles and over-sized spiders.

You know why you think it's not a school? Because we haven't learned how to look at it.

Let's learn it together then.

Just take a chair. No one will stop you. Go ahead, the easiest one, no one will mind.

Just look. Find a child who is not doing anything. O.K. You've found one?

Just keep looking. See. . .there. . .see the teacher putting his arm around that child and talking to him? See the child going to that pair of scales to weigh some stuff and make notes?

See, see the teacher. He's with a group of students now, who are building something.

Go ahead, have a look. It's a model hydro-electric station, with waterfalls, a river, a turbine, and would you believe it, wires and a small lamp, *giving light!*

The teacher is gone already, and he's reading a story to six kids, sitting on the floor with them. The kids stop him sometimes, and he explains a point or two.

In another corner a student is reading out loud to another small group.

Two students are standing over a globe, they bend over, look closely, and then write something down.

Five kids are playing a game with sticks of different length and different colours. They make notes too.

One girl is lying upside down with hands over ears reading a book by herself. Go back to your chair. Sit down. Close your eyes for fifteen minutes. Just listen for how many conversations you can pick up. Tough, isn't it? Unless you concentrate on one, you can't really hear any specific conversation. That's why nobody is distracted in such a classroom. The kids have learned how to ignore other conversations. Open your eyes. Is the classroom still the same? Strange, isn't it. Kids are doing different things now. At least, it seems that way. It's just that different kids are doing the same things now, except differently. Confusing, isn't it?

But have you noticed the teacher? Seems to be busy somewhere all the time, doesn't he? Busy life, that teaching, hardly time to sit back and relax. He seems to know what goes on though. Sees a fight developing, and settles it. Gets asked a question and finds the right book. Gets asked another question, and repairs the power dam. Gets read to and reads. Helps with writing, and writes. Plays and, would you know it, he even asks students to answer some questions, or show their work to him.

That's all for now. Don't tell me there are no such schools, for I've seen them with my own eyes. Not all of them are successful. That's not surprising, for we adults have to learn how to organize schools for learning, and it will take some time. But some are succeeding, including one Christian school I know — it is *that* one I just described! It's the happiest school I know of.

We shall not explore all aspects of it either. We couldn't, for it will take some years of experience before

138

we can reflect on it with sufficient authority. But we should ask some questions.

1. Where is the curriculum in such a school?

The curriculum is present whenever the teacher presents educational materials and questions in specific sequences and for specific purposes. But instead of presenting the same material, in the same form to the whole class, and asking the same sequence of questions of every student, he finds the kinds of materials, and phrases the questions the right way, so that *all* students can grapple with the learning problems.

There are millions of materials teachers could bring to classrooms, and there are millions of questions a teacher could ask. But it is the vision of life of that teacher which will determine what he will choose to bring into a classroom.

That is why only Christian schools could safely undertake this kind of schooling. For only Christian teachers have access to the right kind of tool, the right vision of life, the stance which reflects accurately the truth of creation. Only a teacher deeply sensitive to how all of life hangs together in created unity, confessing that God's Word holds for it all, can choose the right kinds of materials and questions so that life in the classroom accurately reflects the reality outside of it. No humanist can make this kind of school work, for humanists must forever present curricula which are distortions of reality.

2. And where is teaching in such a classroom?

Teaching is happening when a teacher constantly surrounds each child – sometimes singly, sometimes in groups, sometimes as the whole class – with the kind of materials and questions for which the child is ready. It is of no use at all to present a child with a task he is unable to perform, because he is not ready for it yet. A teacher sensitive to children's *needs,* and adept at discerning when learning occurs, will constantly seek contact with all his

Adrian Peetoom

students, to find out whether they are fruitfully busy. And when his students are not, he will interfere. Sometimes this interference will take the place of presenting a different task to the student, sometimes it will take the form of working with the student, of finding other students to work with him, sometimes it will take the form of prodding. Sometimes – it depends on the child – he will put into words what he expects a student to do, sometimes – it depends on the kind of student – he will not.

3. And where is the discipline in such a classroom?

Discipline is never its own justification. The early Nazi soldiers were the best disciplined ones in the Second World War, but the purpose of their discipline was bestial and satanic. Discipline should lead to discipleship.

In such a classroom, children are surrounded by tasks which are within their powers. It is of course the teacher who sets the task, for if he is sensitive to children he will be aware that children can usually tackle much more than they think, and therefore he will constantly give them challenging tasks. Nevertheless he will never give them a task they cannot fulfill.

In such an environment children will be happy learners, and they will discipline themselves. They will probably show up for school much earlier than nine o'clock, perhaps ignore recess and certainly some will have to be sent home at the end of the day, long after school is officially closed.

4. Is it possible to organize schools for learning? If it isn't, we can't have schools, for schools *are* places for learning.

5. Can you be an instrument so that Christian schools develop this way? Only you can answer that question.

5

THE CHRISTIAN SCHOOL IN SOCIETY

Towards Implementing the Vision of Christian Education

by John A. Olthuis

Children have long been treated as society's most important natural resource. Since the industrial/business sector requires the most finished products, it has most often determined how the raw materials should be processed.

Education for the Industrial Society

Author Alvin Toffler writes in his book *Future Shock* that

"Mass education was the ingenious machine constructed by industrialism to produce the kind of adults it needed. The problem was inordinately complex. How to pre-adapt children for a new world – a world of repetitive indoor toil, smoke, noise, machines, crowded living conditions, collective discipline, a world in which time was to be regulated not by the cycle of sun and moon, but by the factory whistle and the clock.

"The solution was an educational system that, in its very structure, simulated this new world...The whole idea of assembling masses of students (raw material) to be processed by teachers (workers) in a centrally located school (factory) was a stroke of industrial genius. The whole administrative hierarchy of education, as it grew up, followed the model of industrial bureaucracy. The very organization of knowledge into permanent disciplines was grounded on industrial assumptions. Children marched from place to place and sat in assigned stations. Bells rang to announce changes of time.

"The inner life of the school thus became an anticipatory mirror, a perfect introduction to industrial society. The most criticized features of education today – the regimentation, lack of individualization, the rigid systems of seating, grouping, grading and marking, the authoritarian role of the teacher – are precisely those that made mass public education so effective an instrument of adaptation for its place and time.

"Young people passing through this education machine merged into an adult society whose structure of jobs, roles and institutions resembled that of the school itself. The school child did not simply learn facts that he could use later on; he lived, as well as learned, a way of life modeled after the one he would lead in the future." (pp. 400-401)

This book's four preceding chapters present quite a different view of the child, education and society – the view that a child is God's gift, and that he is to be led by teachers and community to serve God and fellowman in all societal relationships. Christian day school education has been pictured as a system with the task of preparing children to serve the coming of God's Kingdom in the industrial zone as well as in all other segments of society.

Christian Responses in the Past

In this essay we want to discuss the difficulties connected with the emergence of a Christian educational system in our society. To grasp the dimensions of that difficulty, we begin with a brief look at how the Christian community reacted to the emergence of the school system Toffler has just described. Historically we find that other sectors of society (state, cultural agencies, family, and church) consented to the school being used in this manner, seemingly on the basis of the principle of "what's good for

General Motors is good for society." A master/servant relationship has existed between the industrial sector and the school. The only groups in society that expressed some difficulty with this relationship were the Christian church and the Christian family. But this "difficulty" was never stated in a truly radical way which questioned the fundamentals of that master/servant relationship between industry and school. As we shall discover below, the different responses generally given by Christians varied somewhat, but there was seldom a questioning of whether the school should indeed prepare students to fit into the industrial society. This "compromise" response is more understandable when we realize that the Christian community struggled for a clear understanding of the relationship in a political climate which endorsed the industrial use of the school as a matter of principle. Danton, one of the leaders of the French Revolution, stated in 1791 that "It is time to establish this important principle: children belong to the Republic before belonging to parents." On the basis of this principle, the state-determined schools should be used for the welfare of the industrial sector, which in turn advances the interests of the state.

Within this context most Christians affiliated with what have now emerged as the main-line Protestant denominations. They decided that the school had no further obligations to assist the church and the Christian family. Christianity, they concluded, was a private matter for church and family; so long as the state schools refrained from explicitly demeaning Christianity they could not be faulted. Other Christians, like those affiliated with what are now known as the more fundamentalistic and evangelical denominations, decided that the public school should also be used by the Christian church and Christian family to promote Christian moral virtues – in addition to serving society.

John A. Olthuis

Now that it is becoming so painfully obvious that the so-called public schools are no longer – if in fact they ever were – promoting Christian moral virtues, many who chose this alternative are either moving in the main-line direction or casting an eye in the direction of Christian day schools, which in turn have developed in two distinctly different ways. Some have simply added a Christian atmosphere to the list of concerns a Christian community should have. Within such a Christian atmosphere so-called "secular" and so-called "sacred" learning both take place. The requirement of a Christian atmosphere results in an isolated Christian academy. Other Christian schools decided to educate the child to assume his Christian responsibilities in every area of life according to the unique requirements of each life relationship. These four different educational choices are in turn distinct expressions of four divergent views of the relationship between Christianity, school, and society.

The "Sell-Out" View

The choice of the main-line Protestants is based on the conviction that the natural world (politics, education, business, the arts, and so on) is basically untouched by the fall into sin; so therefore, Christians and unbelievers have a common task to develop it, and young people from all faith communities (both Christian and atheist for example) should receive an identical education to prepare them to participate in an identical manner in building and developing the natural world. This educative process takes place in the public school. This view might well be labeled the "sell-out" view, because it sells out certain areas of life to one or another variant of the humanist religion.

Towards Implementing the Vision of Christian Education

The "Sprinkling" View

The position of the more evangelical Christian is that the natural world is bad and irredeemable, so Christians can only go into it when it's necessary, such as for economic reasons, and when they do go into it, they can't change it; it's basically irredeemable, so the best they can do is hope to change some people in it. The school, therefore, must teach Christian ethics and standards of conduct to students so that they can change the world. This view may be labeled the "sprinkling" view; sprinkling a little Christianity on top of a basically bad world will somehow make the bad world better through individual contributions, even though that world itself will not and cannot change.

The "Hothouse" View

The choice of the atmosphere-conscious Christian is based on the conviction that the world is not only bad and irredeemable, but it is so bad that it has a negative influence on Christians and in particular on Christian young people. These young people must therefore be isolated from the world. This view may be called the "hothouse" view, because it isolates and educates young people in an artificial manner.

The "Kingdom" View

The fourth view is based on the conviction that the world and everything in it was affected both by the fall into sin and by the resurrection of Jesus Christ, and that Christians have a corporate responsibility to claim all areas of life for Jesus Christ. This view rejects the assumption that the world is good in itself, or bad and irredeemable, and holds that the Scriptures teach us the world was cast into sin by the fall, but the possibility for redemption is secured through the resurrection of Jesus Christ. Hence, the Christian school must train the child in the total Kingdom perspective. This means training the child to do everything, including his politics and his business, in an integrally Christian manner.

The first four chapters have attempted to make a case for the "Kingdom" view, stating in chapter one that this view is biblical; in chapter two that historically things have gone wrong and we must seek to correct that wrong development; in chapter three that we need a curriculum designed to take the child through a rehearsal for living total Christianity; and in the fourth that we need an approach to the child that will lead (and not pull) him through the curriculum, so that upon graduation he will work responsibly to build a totally new way of life in Christ.

The Search for Confessional Unity

Our attention must now be turned to the future of Christian education in our society. The possibility of reaching a consensus on societal and educational goals depends not on how kind, understanding, tolerant, patient, and long-suffering we are with one another, but rather on whether we can come to more unity on the basic confessional question of what we mean when we say that we must love God and our neighbors as ourselves. If we can come to some agreement on the confessional level, then, although it will take kindness, understanding, tolerance, patience and long-suffering, I believe we can also come to some agreement on societal goals, educational goals, curriculum, an approach to the child, and so on.

The Christian community must attempt to resolve its own crisis at a time when the deepening crisis of the humanistic world is undermining and chaing humanistic educational systems as well as other humanistic cultural systems. Toffler's book is of some assistance in identifying the current stage of the humanist crisis. In a word, the stage is one of uncertainty, and uncertainty breeds fear and chaos. The world is uncertain about its future. In past generations the question of what the future would be like was answered with an enthusiastic "Bright!". Today it's answered with a dark, foreboding "We don't really know." This uncertainty has shaken the humanist's faith in his society. His faith rests in himself and in his fellowman — faith that together they can erect and control man's destiny, his future, and his society. However, the industrial era, so painstakingly put together by the "progressive" society, changed into a monster. Today this "progressive" monster has turned on its creator, smacking its lips in anticipation of devouring everybody and everything in its path. As awarness of the crisis strikes North America, humanists are reacting in a number of ways:

a. Some advocate a *return to the good old days* of the industrial era; more law and order, more free enterprise, more discipline, more morality. The industrial system is okay, and so is the educational system based on it, but sinful people have made a real mess of things, so the people, *not* the system, must be changed.

b. Others say, "Let's *just live today,* because we don't know about tomorrow. We've lost control of society as a whole; it's losing its hold on us as individuals (as it disintegrates), so we can now control our own lives."

c. A third group realizes that we can't turn the clock back to the good old days; we must be concerned about tomorrow and about regaining control of society. So we must do two things. First, we must attempt to *cope with change*; second, we must *set new goals* for society, goals that we consciously set out to meet.

The important point is that all of these reactions express themselves educationally. The first reaction – "back to the good old days" – is present in renewed zeal for the traditional conditioning school. The "good old days" people believe in the industrial society; believe it should and will be preserved; and believe that the school should continue stamping out the replacement parts for that system (a la Toffler). In fact, they claim that greater regimentation and discipline are necessary to counteract the current apathetic attitude of many people in the industrial enterprise. Secondly, the reaction of the "free-livers" reaches a climax in the "free school" where children are encouraged to do whatever they please. Thirdly, the "copability" option is observable in schools advocating a less rigid curriculum, more learning through experience and more freedom for the child. In essence, more variety in meeting educational goals. This has also come to expression, I believe, in the more "informal" approach expressed, for example, in certain community schools run by local citizens' groups.

There is a very obvious development towards a wide variety of educational systems designed to meet the needs of the future. Our society is changing so quickly and in so many ways that it is almost impossible to predict the future. The educational trend is accordingly moving away from turning out students to fit into a society we know will evolve, to training students to cope with whatever kind of society does indeed develop. The struggle is still gaining momentum between the old traditionalists (those who want the school to reflect the current industrial model), and the more innovative (the informal educationalists) who want to train students to cope with whatever future industrial model will emerge. In Philadelphia. Pennsylvania, for example, "old traditional" mayor Rizzo fired new traditional school superintendent Schedd after winning the election (many believe because of his promise to fire Schedd eight seconds after he was elected). But in Louisville, Kentucky the new traditionalists seem to be gaining control of the educational system. The point is that this turmoil and uncertainty in determining educational goals is a reflection of the current state of uncertainty in determining societal goals.

In addition to coping with the present situation, the humanist is also taking definite steps to regain control of his runaway society to shore up his disintegrating faith. The humanist is deeply interested in a future when his faith will be secure. Because of this concern with the unseen, futurology has become the "in-thing." Governments, corporations, schools – just about every group (including some churches) – have departments of futurology. The MacDonald's hamburger chain has a big hamburger waterbed where executives can lie for days while thinking about the future. If humanists can agree on the kind of society they want, or perhaps the kind they need for survival, in the same way that they came to general agreement at the advent of the industrial era, then I believe the public school system will once again solidify into the kind of machine needed to process raw materials for the new society. If, on the other hand, humanists can *not* agree on societal goals, then they will end up with three or four different educational systems, which in turn will lead to a continuing crisis as different thought communities struggle for societal leadership, and eventually perhaps to a totalitarian society or the breakdown of the present society into self-contained societies. As an example of the difficulties the humanist community experiences, we know that the John Birch mentality adovcates a society that is vastly different from the kind being suggested by certain left-wing humanists.

Adaptation or Challenge

But this humanist crisis is paralleled by an analogous crisis in the Christian community. The critical question facing the Christian community is whether it will resolve its own crisis in the same way it coped with the decisive turning point at the dawn of the industrial era. Then Christians responded by reacting to that new kind of humanist community as it evolved. The alternative would be to add to the humanist crisis by demanding that they also cope with a growing community newly dedicated and committed to a totally Christian way of life. In effect, the Christian community must now determine what kind of society it believes should evolve for the peace and well-being of North America.

I believe that the basic decision of the Christian community must be made at the confessional level of life where we state that we should love God and our neighbor as ourselves. This is the crucial level because it determines the view we will hold of the relationship between Christianity, school and society, and hence the kind of Christian school system we believe should evolve in North-American society. We have already taken a brief look at some different conceptions of education and the different worldviews out of which these concepts have developed. We must now understand that these worldviews in turn are rooted in two different interpretations of the basic commandment to love God and my neighbor as myself and variants of these two interpretations.

Traditionally, the "conservatives" have stressed the "love God" part of the commandment almost to the exclusion of the "love my neighbor as myself" part. The "love my neighbor as myself" part of the commandment has been reduced to a moralistic and individualistic duty to witness to my neighbor. This personal witness is not of the manner in which love of God might come to expression in a different way in each area of life, but of the necessity of my neighbor coming to a confession of faith in Jesus Christ, of being *saved,* and then of accepting his responsibility to save another soul. This is basically because *the world itself is understood to be evil and hence irredeemable.* The presumed evilness of the world has led some Christians to hold the view that public schools should teach morality, and many others to decide for isolationistic Christian schools.

On the other hand, the traditional "liberal" choice has been to stress the "love my neighbor as myself" part of the commandment. Hence *social liberals try to express love and concern for others without worrying too much about* how *God wants that love to be expressed.* The more biblical position is that both parts of the great commandment (that is, to "love God and one's neighbor as oneself") must be confessed and lived out together. *You cannot love God without showing love to your neighbor, and you show love to your neighbor by loving him the way God wants you to.* That means that it is not enough to say to our fellow worker on the job that he should be morally good by not swearing, but we must try to show how love of God comes to expression in the relationship between employer and employee and the meaning of the work itself. In politics, for example, this means that the concept of justice is an expression of politically loving one's neighbor as oneself. This love, then, must be worked out differently in different societal relationships. Such an understanding of the great commandment leads to a Christian school system which seeks to train a child for a total life of involvement according to the unique responsibilities of each of life's relationships. Confessional

John A. Olthuis

agreement is essential to any understanding of, and consensus on, societal educational and curricular goals.

* * * *

Key Roles in the Implementation of Total Christianity

Having shown the types of confessional choices different parts of the Christian community have made in the past; having also attempted to indicate the crucial importance of choices at the confessional level; and having argued for a confessional choice assuming the unity of the command to love God with all our might and our neighbour as ourselves; in the last part of this essay I will concentrate on four goals:

to indicate what implementation of this confession I believe must be undertaken in societal sectors other than the school;

to show how Christian schools should implement this confessional vision;

to outline what the Association for the Advancement of Christian Scholarship (AACS) and its Institute for Christian Studies (ICS) are doing to help implement this vision; and

to suggest what each of us can do to help.

The Role of Other Societal Institutions

First then, what implementation of this confessional vision — the integral confessional vision of "love God and my neighbor as myself" — must be undertaken in societal sectors other than the school?

Towards Implementing the Vision of Christian Education

I believe that activities must be begun and continued simultaneously in a number of areas. These activities should all be designed to show love for God and fellowman. All should be designed to bring service and shalom to our society. Many of these activities may only be begun by this generation, but hopefully they will be continued by the next generation of Christianly-trained people. These activities must all be attempts to build alternative institutions as visible signposts of the coming of Christ's Kingdom. These activities must be visible, that is to say, they must be *public* contributions. Christians must *do* love; we must believe we have a *contribution* to make in our society. We must make that contribution by doing Christian art, doing Christian music, doing Christian writing, doing Christian filmmaking, doing Christian industrial work, doing Christian politics, doing Christian math, and so on.

In each of these areas we must begin with nothing much more than the confessional vision of "love God and our neighbors as ourselves" and as we begin we must engage in three things simultaneously.

(1) The *development* of Christian ideas. Christian educational and research institutions play a crucial role here.

(2) The *communication* of ideas. Christian journalists, broadcasters, and filmmakers are indispensable for this task. We must communicate our ideas to the world.

(3) *Implementation* of ideas in action projects. We must *do* the Christian art, the Christian writing, the Christian filmmaking, the Christian political action, and so on. But we must do it all on the basis of a development of Christian ideas. The doing of Christian work will then generate new ideas which must be developed, communicated and in turn lead to the next steps in Christian action. This is our reasonable service. It's work in faith, not knowing how far we'll get and not being too

concerned about it because it's in God's hand; our task is simply to proceed in faith and to work with enthusiasm.

One of the alternative institutions we must begin building is a Christian political system — a Christian concept of the state and its relationship to other societal structures. I want to say a few words about the crucial role of the state and more particularly of the development and implementation of the Christian concept of the state if public Christian contributions have to be made in other areas of life. At present the state in North America discourages the making of public Christian contributions — or indeed the *public* contributions of any community that expresses different societal (and hence different educational) goals. Therefore, the emergence of Christian activity in alternative Christian institutions is made extremely difficult by the state. Some of the sanctions imposed are the following: There's no "public" money for Christian counselling services, no "public" money for the pluralization of probation services or Christian schools.

The Amish provide a good case in point. The educational views of the Amish in Wisconsin were recently considered in a case before the Supreme Court of the United States, and it decided on behalf of the Amish, but the issues at stake have not be resolved. Wisconsin, like most states and Canadian provinces, has compulsory school attendance laws which can be met by attendance at either public or so-called "private schools." The Amish, however, believe that all higher education (above grade eight) constitutes a deterrence to salvation and a violation of the requirements of an agricultural community separate from the world. They object to any formal education after the eighth grade and instead train their children in the skills of the agrarian society. The Wisconsin Trial Court said that they were guilty of violating compulsory attendance laws. The Supreme Court of Wisconsin said they were not, because public school education would make Amish life impossible, and that the State has no "compelling interest" on the basis of which the State's view should take precedence over that of Amish parents.

The issues raised in this case are of considerable interest for our present discussions. The Amish state, "We do not share the majority view of the relationship between the school and society, because we do not share the majority view of society." They say instead, "Our way of life is to build our agrarian society — totally self-sufficient and isolated from the world. Our educational goal is to educate our young people to preserve our society and this means no formal education after grade eight." The state of Wisconsin on the other hand argues that the Amish cannot do this because participation in the state educational system, at least to the compulsory age of sixteen is essential to the survival of society. It's essential, they argue, (a) to preserve the political system, (b) for economic survival, and (c) for the socialization of children. We are faced head-on with two conflicting claims. The Amish claim "Our view of education is essential for the preservation of our way of life." The state of Wisconsin claims "Our view of education is essential for the preservation of our way of life."

At present the established view of life maintains itself in part by imposing sanctions (economic and other) on other ways of life that come to particular societal expression. The escape valve for the established society is to declare that every contribution which it judges does not advance the publicly established way of life is private because it advances private (that is, other than the established way of life) ways of life. And as long as those private ways of life don't emerge as threats to the public established way of life, they will be tolerated, albeit discouraged by economic and other sanctions. But when a so-called private view threatens the established view of life, there is real anxiety and a clamp-down. This is, for instance, what has happened over the past few years to the "Left" in the United States.

Here we must ask if the Christian community, despite the sanctions imposed against it, will emerge as the next public threat to the established way of life. As part of that emergence a new concept of the state must be advanced. It must be the concept that the state's task is not to advance or to give a monopoly to one set of goals found in its thought communities, but rather to set the conditions within which all public views are treated alike; in which all public views are given the freedom not just to be expressed in ideas, but also in concrete reality. The state has the task, then, of setting the ground rules within which all thought systems can freely come to expression. This is the concept of *structural pluralism,* a model of which might include three or four different school systems, all operating under the umbrella of certain state regulations that apply to them all, but do not affect the internal operation of each system.

So in addition to the emergence of alternative contributions, and alternative institutions in other areas of life, Christians must actively suggest and build an alternative to the present concept of the state. This is of crucial importance. I believe it could lead to one of three developments in North American society:

(1) As Christians emerge publicly, their very presence will demonstrate that Christianity is not only a private but also a *public* religion; in response the present totalitarian system might well smother it by imposing all kinds of sanctions, for Christianity will then emerge as a threat to the established way of life. The totalitarian system would attempt to maintain itself regardless of whether it was a Nixon, a McGovern, a Wallace, a John Bircher or a radical socialist in power. These pseudo-options would differ from one another only in the extent of *private* freedom each of

them decided to grant to a "private" Christianity. As a Christian worldview (or some other than the established worldview) emerged as a threat to the established way of life, that way of life would attempt to smother it. This is one possible result of the emergence of public Christianity.

(2) The second possibility is that Christianity might emerge with such healing force in humanist society that it could not be easily smothered. This could lead to the adoption of the concept of structural pluralism at the political level. This might mean that a new political system could be adopted which would permit each thought system in the society to operate freely, giving concrete institutional expression to its basic beliefs. This would mean the emergence of a number of public school systems each characterized by a different worldview, the emergence of a number of different labour unions, all treated alike, the emergence of Christian probation services, the emergence of Christian filmmaking guilds; all would be treated as *public* contributions and would be financed by the funds of those people in the society who supported the emergence and development of a particular institution.

(3) The third possibility is that the now-dominant society might break down into three to four self-contained societies. If the emergence of public Christianity were too strong to be smothered but not strong enough, so to speak, to result in the concept of structural pluralism, Christians may well be told that they should go into a corner of the country and build their own nation. This has already happened, of course, to a certain extent with the Amish on the one hand and the Black Muslims (and other black movements) on the other; the latter want a certain section of the U.S. set aside in which blacks can erect their own nation.

John A. Olthuis

We should not speculate too much about these possibilities. We need only be aware of the possible reactions as Christianity (hopefully) becomes a public option.

The Role of Christian Schools

Second, what role should Christian schools play in the implementation of this vision?

I believe that Christian schools have a crucial role to play in the emergence of public Christianity because they must educate the persons who will make it possible. Since different educational goals reflect different societal goals, a different Christian educational system will be needed to adapt to the evolving humanistic culture than to support the emergence of public Christianity. Christian schools provide the link between the present society and the possibilities for the emergence of a different type of society. The last three chapters of this book have been devoted to discussing how an educational system, dedicated to the emergence of a different type of society, should be structured. A different curriculum has to be built, a different approach to the child has to be practiced, etc. So the Christian school plays a vital role within the total societal context. If Christianity is to emerge publicly, Christian schools must dedicate themselves to training young people who can take up that challenge.

The Role of the AACS/ICS

Third, what are the Association for the Advancement of Christian Scholarship (AACS) and the Institute for Christian Studies (ICS) trying to do in this context? Let me quote from the AACS Constitution:

Towards Implementing the Vision of Christian Education

> The purpose of the Association shall be to undertake or promote whatever activities it shall deem conducive to the development of scripturally directed learning and scholarly enterprise, and particularly to establish, control and develop a Christian university, and in these ways to equip men and women to bring the Word of God in all its power to bear upon the whole of life.

This statement of purpose is a confessional response to what we believe God's Word calls us to do in higher education. The AACS helps the people of God prepare for their public contribution via three main avenues — through the development of ideas, through the communication of these ideas, and through the implementation of ideas in action projects. Looked at in terms of the framework outlined above, the Association's missions can be broken down into three stages:

1) The Development of Ideas

The main project of the Association is the Institute for Christian Studies, a graduate level research centre located in Toronto, Canada. The Institute has a dual purpose: first, the Institute community is attempting to further articulate a general philosophical systematics and to develop philosophies of the special sciences — both in the Spirit of Christ as affirmed in the preamble and educational creed of the AACS. Secondly, in so doing it helps equip students with basic ordering insights necessary to understand the various fields of learning in the totality of human life. The student is led to acknowledge Christ as the true way of learning and living.

The Institute program for the development of ideas is carried out in a number of ways, including discussions and seminars, sustained research, student/faculty interchange, original publications, translations, and inter-faculty seminars with other Christian institutions of higher learning. Besides this, the Institute often sponsors summer workshops and seminars in special areas of interest in which outstanding Christian scholars join the Institute staff to struggle with issues at a foundational level.

2) The Communication of Ideas

The Association has always put a high priority on the communication of ideas through the print media. Publications have included scholarly, semi-scholarly and popular books, booklets and pamphlets. The Christian Perspectives include H. Evan Runner's *Relation of the Bible to Learning* and *Scriptural Religion and Political Task,* Hendrik Hart's *Challenge of Our Age,* Calvin Seerveld's *Christian Critique of Art and Literature,* and Peter Schouls' *Insight, Authority and Power.* More popular books are found in the Discovery Series which include *Hope for the Family* by Arnold De Graaff and others, *Out of Concern for the Church* and *Will all the King's men.* These and many other publications are now available through Wedge Publishing Foundation in Toronto, an organization set up to disseminate scripturally-directed ideas throughout the world.

Besides these methods of communicating ideas, the AACS has engaged in the organizing of study conferences throughout North America to provide biblical guidance for scholars, students, and the general public. These study conferences have proven to be one of the most important sources of new insight and communal sharing which the Association has undertaken. AACS-sponsored conferences are being supplemented by sharing with other groups and movements in their conferences through exchange of speakers and participants.

The chapters for this book were first delivered on the Discovery lecture series which was given in communities in many parts of Canada and the U.S. through personal speakers and videotaped TV productions. This growing outreach has provided invaluable interaction and communication with a far-flung constituency. The aim of the Discovery series is to provide the results of biblically-attuned scholarship in language that can be understood by the general public.

3) The Implementation of Ideas in Action Projects

The AACS has long encouraged the formation and development of other Christian agencies, associations and organizations giving a witness in diverse fields of contemporary life. To mention only a few, the Association has worked to provide support for the Christian Labour Association of Canada (CLAC), the Committee for Justice and Liberty (CJL), a Canadian Christian political and civil rights movement, the National Association for Christian Political Action (NACPA) and the Christian Government Movement (CGM) in the U.S.A., Wedge Publishing Foundation, Vanguard Magazine, Patmos Workshop and Gallery, the Christian Farmers Federation, the Coalition for Christian Outreach in Pittsburgh, Pennsylvania, and Young Life in North America, as well as other organizations and movements in England, Australia, South Africa, and Lebanon.

One of the areas in which the Institute staff and students are active is that of educational theory. This work is tested and refined in more practically-oriented summer workshops which are co-sponsored by the Association with other Christian educational institutions for the development of a more competent corps of Christian day school teachers, and to fashion new curriculum materials which provide education for public Christianity. So the Institute program in the development of ideas is supplemented by various AACS projects designed to make these ideas fruitful in the life of the Christian community, and to give feedback to theorists working at the Institute. In all of these ways the AACS and ICS are attempting to assist the Christian community.

John A. Olthuis

Your Role

And fourth, what can you do?

This is always a difficult and agonizing question. But I think that together we can come up with some answers. We must first search our own hearts. Have we religiously committed ourselves to loving God and our neighbors as ourselves? Have we answered God's call to build the ark? That's the crucial question. If we have, then we know where we're headed religiously. We have chosen the new way of life; we've decided to build the ark; and religiously we've decided to disentangle ourselves from activities that reinforce the established way of life. But to live out that confession, we must begin to disentangle ourselves from our present "construction jobs." This is much easier for those of us who are just entering life's work than for those who are in established jobs. Ours will probably be the generation of transition. The older generation will disentangle themselves as much as they can, and in so doing will be able to give money, encouragement and support to the younger generation who are already at work building the ark.

You know, it was not easy for Noah to build his ark. His friends and neighbors laughed at him. The skies were a cloudless blue. And there was Noah building that big boat in his backyard. And that's what *we* must do. Some must build, some must supply the materials, others the know-how and the money, all while we are being laughed at. "Where do you think you're going?" people say. They stand and point their fingers and laugh.

Our task is not only to build that ark but also to train sailors to sail it, and we do that training in Christian educational institutions. We must trust in God that we'll get to take a maiden voyage to we-don't-yet-know-where.

164

Towards Implementing the Vision of Christian Education

In the first place, then, each of us must recommit himself through prayer and dedication to living the new life, not just in a confessional statement but in confessional *living,* building the ark, disentangling ourselves from our present construction jobs, and helping one another to do the same. And as we disentangle ourselves, we need not spend all that much time trying to convince our neighbors that our vision and goals are the right ones. If Noah and his family had spent their time trying to convince others that it was a good idea to build the ark, the ark would never have been built. This disentanglement must come in many ways, disengaging ourselves from present political parties and trying to build a Christian political party; in helping our families and our marriages and our circle of friends to stop serving the established way of life; in short, turning towards the integrally new life style.

What does this mean for Christian education in particular? You will recall our earlier discussion about the crisis of vision in Christian education. You'll also recall my comments that Christian schools must move toward the new curriculum and the new approach to the child. If we are involved with a Christian educational community that we — with our circle of friends and reformational community — judge is not attuned to a total Kingdom approach (and therefore not attuned to a new curricular approach), we must begin building a school system that is. This will be more difficult for some than for others. But if we remain entangled in an educational system that reflects a different commitment; if we continue to say "maybe we can change it," we may well end up the way Noah would have if he had spent his time trying to convince his neighbors rather than building the ark.

In addition, we must remember that education is a task involving many societal spheres, and different persons may be able to advance the cause of Christian education in different ways. For instance, if you are a student who

John A. Olthuis

expects to join an academic team after you receive your BA or BS degree, inquire about the ICS. Whatever you decide, make sure that your scholarly work helps build the new way of life, not the established way of life. If you are a parent, encourage your children to give themselves to this kind of academic enterprise. If you are a teacher, join in the summer curriculum writing workshops and in the other workshops at the Institute and in other situations. And also support the work financially. Become a member of the AACS. Educate yourself by becoming familiar with publications that attempt to communicate the basic ideas of the new way of life. You will be more able to communicate these ideas yourself if you read a magazine like *Vanguard* regularly, and if you read books such as those issued by Wedge Publishing Foundation. If you can write, make you contribute by writing. If you have a gift for filmmaking, or artistic talents, make sure that you communicate the Christian gospel in these ways. At the action level, get involved with supporting organizations like the National Association for Christian Political Action, the Chrsitian Labour Association of Canada, and the Committee for Justice and Liberty Foundation. All these action agencies are crucial, for example, in the development of Christian education.

Conclusion

Finally, it is my hope and prayer that this book may have contributed in some small measure to your understanding of the tremendous task we have in Christian education. May we work together so that the grand vision of the coming of God's Kingdom can find concrete meaning in the very midst of our educational goals, curriculum, and the way we lead our children through the curriculum. May God bless our faithful efforts as we strive to joyfully and obediently build the educational ark.

An Educational Creed

by James H. Olthuis and Bernard Zylstra

Basis Article

The supreme standard for all matters of education shall be Written Word of God, known as the Old and New Testament Scriptures, as it opens our eyes to know the Word of God as the structuring and directing plan for creation and as it leads us to confess Jesus Christ as the Word Incarnate.

Note: Due to the fact that the Church of Christ today almost universally restricts its attention to the *Written* and *Incarnate* Words, a note is in order about the Word of God as the structuring plan for creation. The Scriptures teach us that "by the Word of Yahweh the heavens were made, their whole array by the breath of his mouth. . .He spoke, and it was created, he commanded and there it stood." (Ps. 33:6-9) The Psalmist further testifies that "He gives an order; his word flashes to earth: to spread snow like a blanket, to strew hoarfrost like ashes, to drop ice like breadcrumbs, and when the cold is unbearable, he sends his word to bring the thaw and warm wind to melt the snow. He reveals his word to Jacob, his statutes and rulings to Israel." (Ps. 147:17-19) "Fire and hail, snow and mist, stormy winds fulfilling his word." (Ps. 148:8) And the words of Peter are to the point: "They are choosing to forget that there were the heavens at the beginning, and that the earth was formed by the word of God out of water and between waters. . .But by the same word, the present sky and earth are destined for fire. . ." (Peter 3:5-7; cf.

Hebrews 11:3; Ps. 119:89-96) "Through faith we understand that the worlds were formed by the Word of God..." (Heb. 11:3) The Word of God is thus the very plan, order, or will *for* the creation by which everything was created and by which everything is upheld to this day. (See also John 1, Ephesians 1, Colossians 1, etc.) The Christian Church must recover the fullness and unity of the Word of God. The Word of God is one. But since man's fall, that Word also comes to us Inscripturated and Incarnated. When mankind fell in Adam, it no longer heard and understood the Word. To make it possible again for man to hear and do the Word, and thus live, God gave the Scriptures to enlighten man as to his place, his nature and his task. Finally, in the "last days He has spoken to us in His Son." (Hebrews 1:1) The Word in its unity and in its forms is the Power of God unto life. That Word is "alive and active. It cuts more deeply than any two-edged sword." (Hebrews 4:12)

Some of the other elements that should be part of such an educational creed are the following:

1. *Life.* Human life in its entirety is religion; it is service of God or of an idol. Education is therefore never neutral but unfolds in obedience or disobedience to the Lord.

2. *Creation.* God created the world in all its ways by His Word and upholds it by His Word. The meaning of creation is focused in the covenantal communion of God with man in Christ. In the fall of Adam mankind chose not to have this communion with Jehovah God. This root disobedience is sin.

3. *Scripture.* The Scriptures, the Word of God Written, teach us of God, of His Word which structures creation, of man as God's servant, and of Christ as the Redeemer.

4. *Christ.* Christ, the Word Incarnate, redeems and renews all of life, including education, from the power of sin. Due to sin this reconciliation and renewal of creation will not be completed until that final day when God shall be all-in-all.

5. *Knowledge.* Knowledge of God, of His Word, and of creation, is

the work of the Holy Spirit in man's heart. He sees us in the truth and directs us to educate in accordance with the Word.

6. *Teaching office.* The Body of Christ is called upon to subdue and develop the earth by, among other things, guiding students into a deeper understanding of God's world and its history. Through the execution of this teaching office in the school pupils and students are to attain responsible maturity grounded in the biblical faith so that they can take up their specific responsibilities and vocations in life in a manner pleasing to the Lord.

7. *Scholarship.* The communal pursuit of theoretic thought is also a matter of obedience to the Lord. Research must be initiated in order to develop a systematic account of the structure of creation. In this way man's knowledge can be deepened and his life's activities more meaningfully ordered.

8. *Reformation.* Teaching and scholarship not biblically normed is still teaching and scholarship because the structure of creation is one and holds for all men. Thus, even though their findings and overall perspectives are distorted and fragmented, teachers and scholars who are not committed to faith in Christ can provide a valuable contribution toward understanding creation. However, since unbelief expresses a total spiritual vision, it deeply affects and distorts the direction of education. For this reason, the biblical way of Christian education is to reform the scholarship of those who are not in Christ rather than to annex it in the way of accommodation.

9. *Freedom and responsibility.* Teaching and research, executed in harmony with relevant norms, are free and responsible activities of men called to these tasks. The teaching staff of an educational institution, under the care and supervision of the proper governing bodies, is directly and communally responsible to the Lord for the execution of the educational task. The responsible freedom of the educator and scholar must be protected against any constraint or domination of the state, the industrial complex, the church, or other societal structure.

10. *Curriculum.* The educational curriculum is the unifying framework which ties the teaching staff, the students, and the

subject matter together in the setting of the school. While parents have the responsibility for determining the spiritual direction of their children's education, the body of educators in the Christian community has the office of articulating the content of the educational curriculum.

11. *The child in the school.* The student as an imagebearer of the Lord is a whole person to be guided in the educational process toward responsible maturity in preparing for his calling in the unfolding of creation and the coming of the Kingdom of God. A Christian view of the child in the educational setting rejects the classical curriculum-centered approach since it tends to reduce students to the status of intellectual absorbers of information without paying heed to the individuality of the child. At the same time, since education takes place within the structures of creation, a Christian view of education rejects the child-centered approach in which creation is considered as a chaos without order and in which man is heralded as the creator rather than unfolder of order and meaning. In the curriculum-centered view the teacher's authority becomes an end in itself; in the child-centered view the pupil's freedom is uncurtailed; in a biblical view the authority of the teaching office given by God is for the sake of the freedom and responsible nurture of the pupil.

The basic focus in education is not on the teacher-curriculum — the "subject matter" in the traditional sense — nor on the student. The teaching team of a school, through the unifying curriculum, must guide and lead the pupils so that they come to learn about creation in the context of the all-inclusive nature of the Kingdom of God. In this light the students in the school are not to be taught adjustment to the morality or the prevailing attitudes of our society; instead they should be led to understand the norms which hold for the various sectors of life as normed dimensions of the Lord's Kingdom and Reign in human history. In this way the school takes its place in leading the child to the understanding that life is meaningful if that child assumes his place in society as one of God's representatives.

Towards a Basic Framework for a Christian General Education Curriculum

by John Van Dyk

Note: the following paragraphs are excerpts and adaptations selected from the first two of three papers designed to provide a basis for dicussion about a Christian college core curriculum.

1. I believe that in our study of the general education curriculum we are confronted by two distinct problems:
   (a) a structural problem, involving the nature and the structure of the various disciplines and the relationship among them, and
   (b) a pedagogical problem, involving the order in which certain of these disciplines ought to be presented to the student. This paper attempts to deal with (a) the problem of structure only, leaving (b) the pedagogical side for subsequent discussion. It must be noted, however, that (b) presupposes (a), that is, a discussion about sequence of courses, selection of courses, prime time in terms of student classification, etc., has meaning and will be fruitful only if the framework and interrelatedness of all the academic activities are seen and understood.

2. At the outset we must state our *confession:* the entire cosmos, the created order, was called into existence by the power of God's Law-Word. All creatures, all things, the whole universe in all its diversity and variety is subject to that Law-Word of God. Man as the crown of creation stands before the face of his Maker, called to render all things in the fullness of his life to the Lord in love and obedience. We may picture it like this: God speaks, and there it is — heaven, earth, animals, plants, things, man — a coherently structured universe. Then God speaks to man again: love me and serve me in the totality of your life.

3. The fall of man brought about the alienation from the Giver of life. By turning his back on the Word, man lost sight of the meaning of his existence as well as of the entire creation order. Apostate man stumbles about in the darkness, attempting to find the source of meaning somewhere within the cosmos. In spite of man's fall, the cosmos remained the cosmos; it did not become chaos. Man remained man, the sun kept shining, the structural laws of God's creation kept on impinging themselves upon man's experience.

4. We as redeemed Christians, rooted in the Lord Jesus Christ who *is* the *Word* of God, are called to renewed obedience. Gripped by the power of the Word through the work of the Holy Spirit, we are called and enabled to render full-orbed service.

   The radical redemption through Jesus Christ implies several things:

   — *restored knowledge of God.* Once again we may know Him as the Creator of heaven and earth, the majestic Father of our Lord Jesus Christ.

   — *restored self-knowledge.* Once again we know who we are; namely, creatures called to walk before the face of the Lord, sinners in Adam but redeemed in Christ, children of God, office-bearers and therefore His representatives in His world.

   — *restored knowledge of the cosmos.* The created order is no longer essentially a mystery, but revelation, the work of God's hand, a coherent reality functioning under God's law.

   Through the power of God's Word we *see* God's Word of revelation in its threefold manifestation: (1) the Inscripturated Word which reveals (2) the Word Incarnate, through whom we see again (3) the Word of revelation for creation. All revelation is one, in that it is all revelation of the Word.

5. The history of western civilization — in fact, all of history — presents a picture of man actively working out his God-given cultural task. The Greeks did it in apostasy. They produced a cultural context in which the Christian message — although initially strong — increasingly succumbed to a watering-down process of synthesis. Since the Renaissance the rise of Humanism, coupled with the secularization process, has produced a very sharp anti-Christian mentality which has persisted to this day. Christianity became confined to an area of

Towards a Basic Framework for a Christian General Education Curriculum

church and morality, while all other sectors of life were turned into bastions of Humanism.

6. It needs to be carefully observed that the apostate spirits of western civilization did not merely deny God and reality as created, dependent reality, but actively constructed their own variety of views of the cosmos. In other words, having lost sight of God's creation as revelation, they did not just sit still, but began to postulate all sorts of structures and frameworks. We must remember that the Fall did not abolish the creation *order*. The Greeks, too, were inescapably confronted by that order. Driven by the cultural mandate, they *had* to give an account of the coherence which they experienced. But, without knowledge of God and without true self-knowledge and knowledge of the cosmos, they inevitably twisted that one coherent, God-created cosmos out of shape, producing distortions that gripped the mind of western civilization with religious power. These distorted views of reality were not products of careful, unbiased analysis, let us remember but welled up from apostate hearts.

7. For example, the Greeks, unable to see man as an integrally *religious* creature made to walk before the face of his Lord, believed that man is a combination of two substances; namely, a rational "spiritual" substance, and a material bodily substance. In addition, they thought the creation order was knowable only through a process of theoretic abstraction. The really *real,* they said, is a matter that can be discerned only by careful application of the intellect. Everyday experience is all appearance. In the Middle Ages the Christian theologians, having accommodated the Gospel to Greek philosophy, saw man as a composite, two-story creature. The lower story consists of the rational natural man that the Greeks had postulated, while the top story is the man of faith, product of the grace dispensed by the Church. This view led to the sharp opposition of faith and reason. Modern Humanism sees man as a subjective thinking ego confronted by an objective material world. The result is a "world of matter" and a "world of mind," or a "world of facts" and a "world of values." As far as the educational curriculum is concerned, one result of this humanistic view was a division of scientific activity into *Natureissenschaft* (natural sciences and mathematics, which had dominated modern Humanism from the time of the Renaissance

to the nineteenth century) and *Geisteswissenschaft* (the so-called humanities and social sciences, which developed in the nineteenth century as a reaction to the privileged position of physical science and math).

8. We may compare reality to a big pie. Man, called to cultural activity, must investigate the pie. The academic, scholarly enterprise carries out this investigation in a theoretic way. The various branches of science focus upon various pieces of pie; so to speak. The unavoidable question, however, is the one of who is to cut the pie. The Greeks cut the pie in a variety of ways (for example Aristotle's theoretical and practical sciences). The medievals did it in another way (trivium, quadrivium, theology vs. philosophy, etc.). The modern Humanists go at it in still another way (for example Nature vs. Geisteswissenschaft). The result is a mass of confusion. For example, is history a social science or does it belong to the humanities? Is theology really the "queen of the sciences"? Is logic a branch of mathematics? If so, why is it in the philosophy curriculum? What about ethics? Does it belong to philosophy or to theology? Or is it a science on its own? What about the so-called "behavioral sciences"? What does the term include and exclude and by what criteria? What about psychology? Does it include anthropology? Or is anthropology really sociology? Is aesthetics really a science? Is philosophy essentially a matter of linguistics? Etcetera etcetera etcetera. Why all this confusion? The answer is that the pie is cut in so many different ways. Hence the crucial question becomes one of how we as Christians ought to cut the pie.

9. To say that the pie can be arbitrarily cut is – in my opinion – to fall victim to subjectivism. Man's subjective knowing activity does not determine the variety of knowledge, but God's structure of law. God created things according to their kind. He upholds his ordinances faithfully. Consequently, you can find a certain amount of correct analysis on the part of all the pie-cutters, simply because the pie is God's pie. For the same reason the structure of things can't help but impress itself upon man. That's why mathematics remains essentially mathematics, whether back in the days of Euclid or in today's space age. Mathematics does not become sociology. Again, biology is something other than economics, not because we decide what

Towards a Basic Framework for a Christian General Education Curriculum

the content of biology and economics shall be, but because the coherent created order gives itself to man's analysis in terms of both a biotic and an economic dimension, as well as in many others.

10. The matter of cutting the pie is obviously not the task of any one of the specific sciences. A biologist in his biological work assumes that there is an area called biology, and that somehow it is not the same thing as mathematics, even though he may use math as a tool. The economist is not concerned with protoplasm. The theologian does not take a keen interest in mathematics. Who then cuts the pie? This, I believe, is typically the task of philosophy. For philosophy is precisely that theoretical activity which does not focus upon any one specific piece of the pie, but on the interrelatedness of all the pieces. Does this make philosophy the "queen of the sciences," another tyrant such as theology has been for so long? Not at all, as I shall try to show later on. It *does* mean that we must take the matter of Christian philosophy very, very seriously. In order to do so we must attempt to remove some common misconceptions.

11. One of the most common misconceptions is that philosophy is an ivory-tower kind of thing, remote from reality, irrelevant and totally impractical, engaged in by people who lean back in comfortable chairs and contemplate the issues of life. I believe that this caricature is the product of a combination of secular influence and ignorance. During the first class period of my Philosophy 201 — introductory philosophy — course I asked my students to write down a definition of the term "philosophy." It turned out that 85% of the students did not have the faintest idea about what philosophy really is. This result probably reflects the state of affairs in the Christian academic community at large.

A second misconception is that we don't really need a philosophy because we have the Bible. Consequently, those given to this view don't think much of philosophy. They are willing to tolerate it because of its imposing name and long history. Philosophy is not really practical or scientific; it is believed, and could easily be dispensed with altogether. And why indeed philosophy when we have the Bible? Once again, a misunderstanding of the nature of philosophy is involved;

John Van Dyk

namely, the idea that philosophy is nothing but a general, vaguely-expressed world-and-life view, lacking scientific methodology and precision. And indeed, if this were so, then why philosophy when the Bible clearly presents a world-and-life view? But in fact the need for a Christian philosophy remains a very urgent matter. For example, when it is claimed that the Bible gives us norms for sociology and psychology, then it must be asked if the Bible tells us what sociology or psychology *are* and how these two disciplines are related and how they differ from each other? Does the Bible give us in specific terms the correct understanding of the nature of sociology and psychology? When we look for supposed biblical norms for sociology, are we not already operating with an assumed notion of sociology? In other words, what piece of the pie does sociology represent? Or in still other words, what basic *systematic philosophy* is silently assumed?

12. Secular philosophy can never come to its own in relation to the other sciences because it has twisted the nature of reality out of shape. Within the Christian academic community, however, an entirely different state of affairs prevails – at least, ought to prevail. Within the Christian academic community, philosophy does not have to compete with linguistics or with mathematics or with anything else. Within the Christian academic community, philosophy can and must play a *central* role, in that it is called to deal with the interrelatedness of all the various branches of science. Such a central role, however, is never a *dominating,* queen-of-the-sciences role, simply because Christian philosophy cannot really be Christian philosophy without the aid of the special sciences; that is, it cannot really be Christian philosophy unless it is constantly open to the corrective influence of the special sciences. Christian philosophy is actively interested in the special sciences and seeks to enrich them by an analysis of their coherence. At the same time the various special sciences must aid in this analysis of coherence by seeking to provide information which will help philosophy to work out this interrelatedness. In this way philosophy seeks to be a servant for all scientific endeavor while seeking to formulate a framework which gives meaning and structure to the entire academic enterprise. This interacting, integrating, communal kind of scholarship and reflection involving philosophy and all the special sciences can

Towards a Basic Framework for a Christian General Education Curriculum

come to its fullest expression only in a Christian academic community which is committed to subjecting the fullness of life, including theory, to the Kingship of Jesus Christ.

13. It is the communal task of philosophy and the special sciences to cut the pie correctly. Only after this has been done can there be opportunity to tackle the problems of curriculum in a meaningful way. Much work already has been done in the development of a truly Christian philosophy. I am referring to the Philosophy of the Cosmonomic Idea, a philosophy growing out of the work of John Calvin and Abraham Kuyper. Instrumental in its development were such scholars as Dooyeweerd and Vollenhoven of the Free University of Amsterdam. The terms "Cosmonomic Idea" has reference to the Christian confession of a created order (*cosmos*) functioning under the law (*nomos*) of God. As a personal note I wish to state that after initially rejecting it, and subsequently searching for a meaningful alternative, I have come to regard the Philosophy of the Cosmonomic Idea as the most significant development in Christian thinking since the Reformation.

14. The theory of modality, integral to the Philosophy of the Cosmonomic Idea, is of prime importance for cutting the pie. Obviously time and space prevent me from going into detail, so I shall confine myself to some brief observations.

   "Modality" refers to law spheres, that is, the *law*ful conditions which allow the coherent creation order to manifest itself in various modes. The law spheres together form one unbreakable coherence (explained in terms of sphere universality), while yet at the same time no one law sphere can be reduced to another (explained in terms of sphere sovereignty). As such the theory of modality stands radically opposed to all forms of modern subjectivism (which reduces the meaning of reality to merely man's subjective experience of it), radically opposed to all forms of reality fragmentation (medieval nature/grace, modern "world of mind" vs. "world of matter"), radically opposed to all those who in historicistic-evolutionistic fashion adhere to the continuity postulate (which ignores sphere sovereignty and therefore in principle allows the development of, for example, organic life from inorganic matter). It is my conviction that the theory of modality within the context of the

177

John Van Dyk

Philosophy of the Cosmonomic Idea could not have been discovered by anyone but a Christian.

15. A brief — and therefore totally inadequate — account of the modal law spheres is necessary in order to be able to demonstrate the implications for the structure of a curriculum. At the present 14 (or 15) law spheres are not isolated "things," but so many ourselves that these law spheres are not isolated "things," but so many ways in which creatures manifest themselves.

The Law Spheres

numerical:	discrete quantity — all existing things can be counted
spatial:	continuous extension — all creatures take up space and are measurable
physical:	movement — recently divided into two law-spheres; namely the kinematic and the energetic
biotic:	organic functions of life — presupposes a physical substrate
psychical:	emotions and perception — presupposes organic life
analytical:	logical differentiation — presupposes perception, i.e. the psychical
historical:	form-giving, technical development; presupposes logical understanding
lingual:	symbolic communication; presupposes the historical in that e.g. languages are formed
social:	presupposes the lingual; e.g. social behavior such as a handshake carries symbolical meaning
economic:	presupposes social intercourse; thrift, distribution of scarce goods.
aesthetic:	harmony — presupposes the economic, e.g. no splashing of color all over
juridical:	justice and legality — presupposes the aesthetic, e.g. justice involves a harmonious balance of interests
ethical:	troth, human loyalty and faithfulness
pistical:	the faith aspect

16. It is unfortunate that for many people familiarity with the Philosophy of the Cosmonomic Idea does not extend beyond a vague idea of "fourteen modalities." This minimal one-sided

Towards a Basic Framework for a Christian General Education Curriculum

acquaintance leads inevitably to all kinds of distortions. The theory of modality cannot be fully understood apart from a careful consideration of (1) sphere universality (the theory of analogy which demonstrates the coherence of the law spheres. Each law sphere reflects the totality of all the law spheres by means of retrocipations and anticipations), (2) sphere sovereignty – mutual irreducibility of the law spheres, and (3) subject and object functions (e.g. a stone functions as a subject in the first three law spheres, that is, the stone functions as a subject in the numerical, spatial, and physical modalities. A plant functions in the first four law spheres; in addition to the three first law spheres a plant is also subject to a biotic law, unlike the stone. Man functions as subject in all law spheres. At the same time subjects can function as objects in other law spheres, for example, a wedding ring is a subject in the first three law spheres, but functions as object in the ethical law sphere, since the *meaning* of the wedding ring involves loyalty and faithfulness. In the sacrament of baptism water functions as object in the pistical law sphere. And so on. An understanding of the subject-object relation in the context of the theory of modality once and for all gets rid of the many distorted notions of subjectivity rampant today.

17. Besides the theory of modality, we need to know something about the theory of individuality. The reason for this will be clear when we remember that, for example, a man is not just an aggregate of modal functions. Let us take a man and an animal as examples. According to the theory of modality an animal functions as a subject in the five lowest modal law spheres, that is, as a subject it is subject to five modal laws (namely, the numerical – one or two, etc. animals; the spatial – it takes up space; the physical – that is, the animal is a physical-chemical structure; the biotic – there are organic functions; and the psychical – the animal perceives). A man functions as subject in all the law spheres, at least fourteen of them, including the first five to which the animal is subject. Does this mean now that man is like an animal and differs only in that he has more subject functions? If this were so we would be right back in Aristotle's

John Van Dyk

anthropology, that is, every creature is uniquely individual, simply by virtue of its creatureliness. Man is man because as a creature (structure of individuality) he was created to be *man,* that is, uniquely man. Man is not some kind of superior animal, but he is made to walk before the face of his Maker in the *fullness* of his existence (that includes all aspects of his temporal existence, including his organic physical aspects).

What then are individuality structures? They are men, animals, plants, and things, as well as events and societal structures. Every individuality structure manifests itself modally. In this context the Philosophy of the Cosmonomic Idea speaks of qualifying functions: for example, a stone is qualified by a physical subject function. A plant is qualified by a biotic subject function. A wedding ring is qualified by an ethical object function. A family is qualified by an ethical subject function, that is, what typifies the family is the promise of abiding fidelity, faithfulness, troth. A state is qualified by a juridical function, the state is called to carry out justice. A school is qualified by a historical, or formative function, educating the children is in essence forming them. It is important to remember that individuality always expresses itself in terms of modality, and that modality can never exist apart from individuals. Modality and individuality are two sides of one coin.

18. We are now ready to look at the curriculum. How are the masses of sciences and disciplines related? We begin with philosophy, not because it is the "queen of the sciences," but simply because it must articulate a theoretical account of the entire creation order. In doing so it articulates a framework for the diversity of academic activity. Keep in mind that philosophy does not impose a system, but that the framework is the product of communal effort on the part of both philosophy and the special sciences. It may be helpful at this point to mention the specific disciplines of philosophy; namely *ontology* and *anthropology.* Ontology concerns itself with the structure of reality, whereas philosophical anthropology focuses upon the structure of man, not merely in his organic aspect (biology), nor in his psychic aspect (psychology), but man as a total creature of God. Ideally speaking we need three kinds of philosophers: (1) systematic philosophers, engaged in further formulation of systematic philosophy; (2) historians of philosophy, engaged in careful

Towards a Basic Framework for a Christian General Education Curriculum

analysis of the history of philosophy; and (3) philosophers of the special sciences, i.e. men who are competent in both philosophy and a special science, e.g., philosophers of history, of physical sciences, of mathematics, etc.

What about the special sciences? We distinguish, in accordance with our philosophical framework, between *modal* sciences and *individuality* sciences. Modal sciences are more abstract than individuality sciences. Modal sciences are engaged in the analysis of one modal dimension as it manifests itself in all of reality. Consequently, in keeping with the variety of law spheres, we list the following modal sciences: theology, ethics, jurisprudence, aesthetics, economics, sociology, linguistics, history, logic, psychology, biology, physics/chemistry, and mathematics (combining the spatial and the numerical). Individuality science utilizes the modal science as it engages in analysis of specific kinds of concrete creational structures. Physics, for example, as a modal science studies the physical aspect of all reality. Astronomy is an individuality science oriented to physics, in that it applies physical theories to specific individuality structures; namely the stars, etc. Another example: jurisprudence is a modal science, in that it concerns itself with the juridical (justice) aspect of all of reality. Political science, on the other hand, is an individuality science in that it studies specifically the structure of the state, an individuality structure. Both modal and individuality sciences are characterized by their theoretic nature. Both involve a great deal of theoretic abstraction. Sometimes a modal science is not easily differentiated from an individuality science. The reasons for this are that (1) the created order is a coherent, interrelated order, and (2) modality and individuality are two sides of one coin. In some cases, not much work has as yet been done with a modal science; for example, in ethics. In other cases, modal sciences have to be recovered; for instance, today logic needs to be rescued from mathematics.

Next in line are what we may call "workshops." In this area we place, for example, the skill courses and practical areas such as method courses and practice teaching. These workshops constitute the arena, as it were, where the academic enterprise meets the fullness of non-academic life.

The structure of the Christian communal academic life can be more conveniently demonstrated by means of a diagram.[1] You will find this diagram on the following page.

19. The proposed structure of Christian communal academic life offers some distinct advantages:

   a. It provides a framework for the entire academic enterprise, in a well-articulated philosophy — admittedly not very evident from this paper — the product of years of Christian communal reflection on the part of both Christian philosophers and Christian specialists in each modal field of scholarship. By adopting such a framework and setting up administrative divisions accordingly, future growth and curricular expansion can be channeled in terms of a complete, well-rounded context.

   b. The proposed framework represents an initial formulation. As such it retains a flexible, tentative character, in need of further investigation by all branches of science. As such it would provide an excellent opportunity to promote communal Christian scholarship.

   c. The proposed framework will enable the Christian community to come to grips with a *well-rounded* general education curriculum. It can provide a picture of the gaps, of what areas need to be emphasized for remedial work, and of what areas must be elaborated or included to insure a *general* education curriculum.

20. As explained above in number 9, the various sciences and disciplines as we know them today are not products of arbitrary human imagination, changeable at will. On the contrary, the creation structure is a coherent structure, which gives itself to human analysis in a variety of law-ordered ways. As such the creation order impinges itself inescapably upon men, who subsequently respond in apostasy or in obedience to the will of the Lord. Apostate man, confronted by created, law-ordered reality, does not see the *coherence* of the creation in Jesus Christ. The secular man will therefore constrict and entangle himself in fragmentation and contradiction. The Christian community, too, after centuries of synthesis and accommodation, has become ensnared in much of this fragmentation.

21. At present, increasing fragmentation and specialization in the secular institutions of learning produces increasing irrelevance. Students do not rebel to satisfy an idle urge. Increasing fragmentation, producing increasing irrelevance, produces

Towards a Basic Framework for a Christian General Education Curriculum

increasing meaninglessness. The loss of meaning lies at the heart of much of contemporary society's troubles. And no wonder, for all things cohere in Jesus Christ! When He is removed from the scene, no true unity of meaning can be discerned.

22. To altogether too great an extent the Christian schools at all levels foster this frustrating sense of meaninglessness. The fact is that in spite of the Bible courses and the chapel exercises, Christian education remains thoroughly infected with secularism. Not only is a very strong hangover of the nature/grace mentality rampant in our schools (which is responsible for the notion that Bible courses, chapel, and moral uprightness constitute the essence of Christian education), but there is also a lack of a unifying perspective which leads to the sense of fragmentation plaguing our institutions. Too often Christian education consists merely of a sequence of unrelated "subjects," with Bible courses and chapel attached.

23. The effort on the part of many members of a Christian school faculty to "integrate Christianity and subject matter" does not necessarily result in an effective, meaningful Christian school. Far too often the attempts are carried out in isolationistic, individualistic fashion, so that within the body of Christ the left hand does not know what the right hand is doing. For Christian education, at whatever level, to succeed, there must be among the teachers not only common convictions and common goals, but a *common view of reality* as well. Radically differing views of reality within the context of a campus inevitably lead to further fragmentation and disintegration. I believe that the importance of this point is grossly underestimated. It seems to me that the Christian community has correctly understood that widely varying views on the inscripturated Word cannot be tolerated. Our creeds and confessions are designed to strengthen the communal bond of outlook upon the Scriptures. When it comes to the Law-Word in creation (general revelation), however, everyone is left to himself; complete individualism takes over. It is my conviction that the success of a Christian school will depend on how effectively its staff members arrive at a communal understanding of the nature of reality, the aspects of which they are all busily teaching.

John Van Dyk

24. At this point we do well to remind ourselves that an undergraduate college, unlike a graduate university, is an *historically* qualified institution. In terms of the theory of modality this means that the college executes a *formative* activity. The university (graduate school), on the other hand, is an *analytically* qualified institution, a place where original research occurs. As an historically qualified institution, the college is a continuation of the elementary school and the high school. The difference is that the college confronts the student with a much greater degree of analysis than either elementary or high school. As a matter of fact, in grade school analysis remains on an elementary level, deepened somewhat in high school. In terms of the modal scale, observe that at early levels of education greater analysis occurs in the lower law spheres than in the higher ones. For example, in grade and high school, a much deeper level of abstraction is achieved in mathematics, physics, and biology than in any other field. It seems to me that it is the college's task to deepen the level of abstraction in those sciences, as well as to extend the deepening of analysis to all the other modal sciences. Since the college is the final stage in the formative process, it ought to present the modal analysis of *all* aspects of reality. I conclude, therefore, that the general education program ought to confront the student with the entire range of the modal sciences.

25. The entire range of the modal sciences in the general education curriculum must reflect the coherence of the creation order. That means that we get away from the idea that the general education curriculum merely presents an opportunity for the students to "taste" of this and that field, so as to enhance his "liberal education." An incoherent smattering of this and that will only contribute to the sense of fragmentation we spoke about earlier. An increasing sense of abstraction and modality should go hand in hand with an increasing integration of encyclopedia. The general education curriculum *must* give the student the sense of wholeness that he needs in order to live a meaningful, integrated Christian life. In order to do this we must for a moment place the entire Christian educational enterprise in a wider context.

26. The wider context I am referring to is the global struggle

Towards a Basic Framework for a Christian General Education Curriculum

between the Kingdom of Jesus Christ and the Kingdom of darkness. Once again we are faced with the problem of secularism in Christian education. The Kingdom of Heaven has too long been identified with the institutional church, with morality, or with a program for winning souls. Such a reduction is often reinforced by Christian education. We need to remind ourselves, however, that our teaching in the Christian school is not limited to a mere presentation of details, but that it entails the clear-cut challenge of the Christian task of asserting the Kingship of Jesus Christ in every area of life. In other words, the curriculum does not do enough if it merely trains students for responsible living. Mere vocational proficiency, combined with moral uprightness, is not enough. There must be a larger framework; namely, the place of the student within the context of the body of Jesus Christ, and the body of Jesus Christ in terms of effective, obedient Kingdom life. The curriculum must integrate to such an extent that our students graduate into an active Kingdom community, ready and able to combat apostate secularism on all fronts. It is imperative that Christian school graduates be equipped with a *program;* namely, the coming of the Kingdom of the Lord on *all* fronts. Nothing less than a *full-orbed* communal Christian witness must be the aim of all our educational endeavors.

27. The general education curriculum, then, provides the integrating factor in the program of the college. The full range of modal sciences should be presented to the student, not as isolated bits of information, but as a reflection of the coherent creation order. As is clear from the diagram above, philosophy plays a crucial role in the curriculum. For, as we saw, philosophy's task is to articulate in a theoretic way the coherence of all modal aspects. Consequently, the philosophy courses in the general education curriculum must demonstrate the coherence among the various disciplines and sciences. Once again, philosophy must do this not in a dominating, queen-of-the-sciences way, but as a servant, open to the corrective influence of all the sciences.

28. We explained that modality and individuality are two sides of one coin, and that as a result modal science and individuality science are closely related. Here again, whatever individuality science is selected for the general education curriculum, it must

John Van Dyk

be taught in such a way that the connection to the modal aspect, and hence the connection to all of reality, becomes clear to the student. A similar state of affairs holds for the skill courses. All skill courses are modally qualified, as the diagram shows. Consequently, skill courses should not merely function as additives to a lot of theorizing, but rather, they should concretely embody a modally-qualified dimension of reality. For example, communication skills ought not to be merely skills, tools in themselves, but ought to demonstrate a lingual dimension of reality to the students.

29. Once the general education curriculum begins to serve as the integrating channel on the campus, new possibilities arise for meaningful majors and minors. It stands to reason that as long as the core program is a conglomeration of unconnected subjects, the areas of specialization will be just that: areas of specialization, that is, little islands adrift in an uncharted academic ocean. However, should the coherence of the modal law spheres become clear, then the interrelatedness of the various sciences will remain a mystery no longer. Consequently, the student will see that their majors and minors are either
    (1) deepening analyses of certain modal dimensions, or
    (2) a more thorough modally understood analysis of certain individuality structures, or
    (3) a concentration on certain modally qualified skills.
    Examples of each: (1) The mathematics major engages in a deepening analysis of certain modal dimensions, namely the spatial and numerical. Without understanding the relation of these aspects to the entire creation order, mathematics for the math major will be only a meaningless game, divorced from concrete reality. (2) An English literature major will delve into concrete structures of individuality, e.g. novels, poems, plays, etc., thus understanding more clearly the aesthetic aspect of reality. (3) The speech major, as he concentrates on his work, thereby acquires an understanding of the lingually qualified nature of speech.

30. If it is true that the general education curriculum presents to the student the full range of modal sciences, then it is equally true that everywhere along the line, the various connections with the major individuality sciences and skills must be conveyed. For

186

Towards a Basic Framework for a Christian General Education Curriculum

example, a general education curriculum math course needs to include computer science (according to the chart, computer sciences are individuality sciences mathematically qualified). Or another example is biology in the general education curriculum; it should show that the various fields of biology, such as ecology, zoology, as well as medical science, athletics, and sports are all biotically qualified. In other words, the general education curriculum gives stature to the basic encyclopedia of the sciences and connected skills. The general education curriculum philosophy course will also need to concentrate significantly on analysis of the encyclopedia.

31. Two questions have probably arisen at this point. First, is the general education curriculum going to be nothing but one great big extended philosophy program? And second, will the presentation of the full range of modal sciences in the general education curriculum not be a practical impossibility? Let us address ourselves to these two questions.

32. The first question that may have come to mind is whether or not the general education curriculum will "degenerate" into nothing but theory and philosophy if indeed we should want to present the full range of modal sciences? The answer will depend somewhat on what you mean by theory and philosophy. It seems to me that the Christian academic community has been influenced by pragmatism to such an extent that not only has practice been very sharply differentiated from theory, but that – this distinction having been adopted – practice is also regarded as superior to theory. In other words, we have lost sight of the integral connection between practice and theory. Space prevents a full elaboration of this point. Let it suffice to say that due to pragmatism and other secular influences, general education curricula and core courses have often deteriorated into nothing but mandatory memorization of irrelevant facts. Presumably a student is "educated" when he has been exposed to a variety of unrelated subjects and has memorized a large number of "facts" – which he promptly forgets two hours after the final examination. Over against this I see a general education curriculum composed of courses which together form the students' insight into the nature of life within the context of a *coherent* creation order as well as the Kingdom task. Is that a

purely philosophic vision? Emphatically not! Yes, philosophy does play a crucial role, as we keep pointing out, but only in terms of a theoretic articulation of *God's created reality*, which is *pre*theoretical and *pre*philosophical in character. What really counts is not primarily the philosophical articulation but the deeper, *religious* understanding of our task and calling as the body of Christ. The Kingdom of the Lord must come! and *that* is not a philosophical matter, but a matter involving the fullness of our lives. The core program, then, is a cooperative effort on the part of philosophy and the various sciences to instill in the student the ability to respond *fully* as an office-bearer in the Kingdom of Jesus Christ. For that, *vision* is necessary, and an ability to discern the spirits. Hence I believe that all the core courses should consist of (1) analysis of the nature of the field of investigation in terms of a common Christian view of reality; (2) analysis of apostate versions and distortions of the field of investigation; and (3) sufficient detailed analysis of the field to allow the student to sense the difference between Christian integration and apostate fragmentation.

33. The second question merits some discussion as well. Is it not technically impossible to present the full range of modal sciences within the confines of a general education curriculum? What about the individuality sciences and skill courses? From the outset let us acknowledge that the implementation of the basic framework is handicapped by a number of considerations, such as available time, personnel, facilities, and finances. We might point out in passing, however, that we do not err when we speak about *what ought to be*. As we plan for the future, whether as college or as high school or as elementary school community, we must work with abundant faith that the Lord will bless as we are obedient and seek His Kingdom first. But how about it? Can all the modal sciences be taught in a general education curriculum? In the first place, let it be clearly understood that when I say that the general education curriculum student should be confronted by the full range of modal sciences, I do not mean that each modal science must be taught in terms of a three-hour course. As I wrote in point 25: "The entire range of the modal sciences in the general education curriculum must reflect the coherence of the creation order." In other words, the *coherence of the creation order* is the important thing. It does not necessarily follow now that the best way to demonstrate that

coherence is by means of three-hour courses in *all* modal sciences. Instead, we can be equally effective by means of certain combinations of modal sciences as well as by allowing options. As a working rule we can say that all combinations and options are acceptable, providing they do not impair growing modal structural awareness.

In the second place, if indeed the staff engaged in teaching the general education curriculum can come to a common understanding of reality, the various courses then reinforce each other to such an extent that equal emphasis need not be placed on every one of the modal sciences.

34. Admittedly this framework will present administrative and practical problems. At the same time it can represent the beginning of a school curriculum which is truly and distinctively Christian. After much more prayer, study, and discussion perhaps it will be possible for us and for others to say that even the Christian school *curriculum* constitutes a powerful witness in a dark and confused world.

Footnotes

[1]The idea for this diagram was given me by Dr. James Olthuis of the Institute for Christian Studies in Toronto. A similar diagram was designed by Dr. Bernard Zylstra (see his "Christian Education Through Social Studies," p. 5). Although the diagrams were constructed independently, the basic idea is to be credited to Dr. Olthuis and Dr. Zylstra.

Also in the Discovery Books series

Will All the King's Men

Will all the King's men be able to put the church back together again?

The answer is a resounding "No!" Only the King Himself will be able to reform and restore His church. But the wonder is that He uses us, His Body, His men, to accomplish the task — when we joyfully and obediently respond to His word by the guidance of the Spirit. *Will All the King's Men* is a response to the Word of God for the worshipping (institutional) church within the witnessing church (the whole People of God in all their activities for the coming Kingdom.)

Will All the King's Men is *Out of Concern for the Church, Phase II.* From the passionate outcries for reformation of the church that constituted *Out of Concern for the Church* (published by Wedge in 1970), the same five authors, John A. Olthuis, Hendrik Hart, Calvin G. Seerveld Bernard Zylstra, and James H. Olthuis, here joined by Arnold De Graaff and John Van Dyk, continue from protest to contribution, from a refusal to accept brokenness as normal, to a positive exposition of a stirring, recovered vision of the total church.

These seven essays were originally given as 1970-71 Discovery lectures on behalf of the international Association for the Advancement of Christian Scholarship (AACS), and have been extensively revised and expanded for publication.

If you have read *Out of Concern for the Church,* you'll find in these pages not a change of heart over the reforms proposed in that controversial volume, but a more mature blueprint for the biblically ecumenical body of called-out-Christians at worship and witness which was already implicit in "Phase I".

Order it direct from Wedge Publishing Foundation, 229 College Street, Toronto 2B, Ontario, Canada or through your local bookstore.